LIFE AND ADVENTURES
OF PETER PORCUPINE

PETER PORCUPINE'S ENLISTMENT

A cartoon by Gillray *satirising* Cobbett's ' *Life and Adventures* '

LIFE

AND

ADVENTURES OF

PETER PORCUPINE

WITH OTHER RECORDS OF HIS EARLY

CAREER IN ENGLAND & AMERICA

VIZ:

LIFE & ADVENTURES	TALLEYRAND : A SPY
THE SCARECROW	FAREWELL TO AMERICA
REMARKS *of the*	A COURT-MARTIAL
PAMPHLETS	A RETROSPECT

BY

WILLIAM COBBETT

KENNIKAT PRESS
Port Washington, N. Y./London

LIFE AND ADVENTURES OF PETER PORCUPINE

First published 1927
Reissued in 1970 by Kennikat Press
Library of Congress Catalog Card No: 77-86005
SBN 8046-0608-0

Manufactured by Taylor Publishing Company Dallas, Texas

THE CONTENTS

Introduction by G. D. H. Cole   1

Preface to the Life and Adventures   11

The Life and Adventures   17

Preface to the Scare-Crow   67

The Scare-Crow   70

Remarks of the Pamphlets lately published against Porcupine   93

Talleyrand : a Spy   120

Farewell to America   124

The Court-Martial   127

A Retrospect   139

Appendix : 145

Notes : 151

THE
INTRODUCTION

By G. D. H. COLE

Everyone who knows his Cobbett enjoys writing about him, just as Cobbett always enjoyed writing about himself. He did it again and again, almost from the moment when he first began to write. The *Political Register* is full of scattered fragments of autobiography, mingled with political diatribes, sage advice about Swedish turnips or American trees, " rural rides " through the English countryside, or disquisitions on the vices of paper money. *Advice to Young Men* is fuller still; there are embedded the story of his courtship and almost fickleness, and a score of other reminiscences, chiefly of his earlier years. Even his " Rustic Harangues," delivered at great meetings of farmers and labourers, are full of such fragments; for Cobbett's way was to present himself to his audience as the flesh and blood embodiment of any cause he wished them to espouse, and his own adventures were his commonest illustrations of the point he was pushing home.

Cobbett's biographers have all drawn largely on this wealth of material presented to them by their subject; but I cannot find that certain of Cobbett's best autobiographical writings have ever, since his own lifetime, been re-printed separate or entire. The piece which stands first in this volume, *The Life and Adventures of Peter Porcupine*, deserves to be read as a whole, and not merely in the extracts which the biographers supply. And it has seemed worth while to collect with it certain other writings of the same period of his career, so as to make a sort of Autobiography of William Cobbett up to the time of his return from America in 1800.

A

It is possible that to some, who know only the Cobbett of *Rural Rides* and *Advice to Young Men*, the opinions expressed in these early writings may come with something of a shock. Used to find his good Billingsgate directed against placemen and financiers, Tories and Whig upholders of privilege, " Parson Malthus " and George IV., they will here discover him abusing, certainly with no less vigour, Tom Paine and the French Revolution, Doctor Priestley and the English Radicals, and their American sympathisers, the Democrats and Republicans. He will find the old Constitution of England, later denounced as corrupt and oligarchic, here lauded as the guardian of order and freedom. He will find George III. a great monarch, and Pitt a minister divinely appointed. Indeed, of almost every political opinion Cobbett held in later years, the opposite is affirmed in his earlier writings with at least equal force of language.

So much is this the case that in these later years Cobbett's enemies had a fine time digging up his inconsistencies, and quoting " deadly parallels " against him. They re-printed his early works and circulated them as if they were new. They made collections of the most ferocious assaults on democracy, and re-published them as *The Beauties of William Cobbett*. They refuted him again and again out of his own mouth. Wherever Cobbett went, he was pursued to the end with these *souvenirs de jeunesse*.

Yet, though the opinions are all different, there is no mistaking the identity of the man. The same hand that wrote about the Bradfords and Baches in 1796 wrote the *Legacy to Peel* in 1835. The *Life and Adventures* are in the same vein as *Advice to Young Men*, which appeared thirty-five years later. Cobbett the Anti-Jacobin and Cobbett the Radical Reformer were very definitely the same person. The opinions change; the attitude remains at bottom the same. For the opinions are the results of circumstance and environment; but the man is throughout himself.

In Cobbett's case, the opinions are important; but it is the man that fascinates or repels. In his own day, he repelled many, both because he hit hard and not always with discrimination, and still more because he seemed to be for ever blowing his own trumpet till he strained his lungs and their ears. To-day, at getting on for a century's distance, we are more tolerant of the big noise Cobbett made, both because we see clearly how much there was to make a noise about, and because it is far easier, in retrospect, to put up with the little ways of the great man. Moreover, we do not care a jot how roundly he abuses Bradford or Franklin, Paine or Priestley, Pitt or Addington, Peel or Brougham. We enjoy the good Billingsgate for its own sake: the *odium politicum* or *theologicum* is not aroused. And there is, above all, no risk that Cobbett may turn suddenly in his grave, and begin roundly abusing us. Dead men edit no *Registers*; we may read in peace.

In this book, we have a Cobbett not quite fully fledged. He was between thirty-three and thirty-seven when he wrote the pieces here collected; but his career as a writer was only beginning. The *Life and Adventures* appeared in 1796, when Cobbett was thirty-three; but his first work was not published till 1794 (or 1793, if we accept *The Soldier's Friend* as his). As a boy, he had the scantiest of educations; he learnt " grammar," and taught himself to write, only in his twenties as a soldier; he seems to have had no idea of writing as a vocation till Dr. Priestley's arrival in America opportunely stung him into pamphleteering. But the stream, once given course, flowed unchecked; and for the rest of his life Cobbett can hardly have passed a day without writing some sort of article, or some bit of a book.

He was incredibly voluminous. For more than thirty years (1802-1835) he edited the *Political Register* and wrote a great part of its contents. He poured out books and pamphlets in a steady and growing stream. During the six years or so of his literary activity in the United States, he wrote enough to fill the twelve substantial volumes of *Porcupine's Works*, besides at least one other book, several volumes of translations, and a great deal of ephemeral journalism. And for the rest of his life he wrote no less, and certainly with no diminution of his powers. He was nearing sixty when he began his *Rural Rides* and published *Cottage Economy*, and sixty-six when his *Advice to Young Men* appeared. And, while his work varies of course in quality, he could never write a dozen lines without some telling phrase or turn that stamped the thing plainly as his.

Cobbett's mastery of good homespun prose appears as decisively in these early writings as in any of his later work. The *Life and Adventures* is as good as anything he ever wrote; *Talleyrand a Spy* as pretty an anecdote as he ever told; *Farewell to America* as satisfying an anathema. I have, indeed, included here two pieces of writing which belong to rather later periods. The account of *The Court-Martial* was written in 1809, and the piece which I have called *A Retrospect* as late as 1820. But compare the manner of the *Retrospect* with that of the *Life and Adventures*, or *The Court-Martial* with *The Scarecrow*. The style is the same—as effective and as forcible in the one as in the other.

Cobbett's style was his own; but the *Retrospect* at least gives us a hint of the influence which helped most to form it. The *Life and Adventures* opens with a quotation from " the celebrated Dean of St. Patrick's "; the *Retrospect* tells us what we might almost have guessed, that *A Tale of a Tub* was Cobbett's first and most cherished book. Swift was not his master; but he learnt much from Swift. Cobbett's weapon was the blunter; but he hit harder by way of compensation.

In order to get the atmosphere of these early tracts, we need to feel how Cobbett came to write them. The story of his own career he can be left to tell for himself; and we can supplement the outline of the *Life and Adventures* with certain records drawn from other sources, especially the *Advice to Young Men*. But these will hardly explain—for perhaps Cobbett never fully realised—how far his early opinions were the product of the circumstances in which he had been placed. Yet it is easy enough to see that only under stress of circumstances did he really develop any political opinions at all.

He was never a theorist, or attracted by theories. He went by what he saw, or felt, around him, reacting directly to his environment and making his generalisations to fit the practical causes he espoused. In later life this made him appear sometimes a misfit among Radical Reformers; it certainly made him, in his early years, quite the most extraordinary Anti-Jacobin of them all.

Let us look back, then, over Cobbett's history up to the time when he wrote his *Observations on Doctor Priestley's Emigration.* A nasty hit, that, in the very title of the pamphlet. Not among Frenchmen alone were there *émigrés*; the Democratic patriot was no less ready to leave his country when things were going badly for him. Cobbett, it is true, was an *émigré* himself; the court-martial proceedings hereinafter described had made England too hot to hold him. But Priestley in exile was vilifying his country and its Government; Cobbett exalted them both.

This patriotism of Cobbett's was instinctive rather than a reasoned belief. Despite his father's partisanship of the Americans in the War of Independence, it is most unlikely that he had developed any political opinions at all before he left home. Nor had he any chance while he was a clerk in Mr. Holland's office. At twenty-one he joined the Army as a private soldier; and then, after a year at the regimental depot at Chatham, he spent more than six years on foreign service. For nearly all this time he was in New Brunswick, mingling either with the soldiers of the garrison or with those " Yankee Loyalists " who had settled there after the American War, and were full of the exaggerated patriotism of the refugee. His attempt to expose the corrupt conduct of his officers had certainly no political motive; he had no idea that the malpractices which he discovered in his own regiment were part of a general system of plunder, equally prevalent throughout the Army. It is, indeed, likely that his attempt to bring the offenders to justice brought him into touch with a group of Radicals in London, and that he took part with them in producing the pamphlet called *The Soldier's*

Friend, which, if not wholly his, bears unmistakable traces of his literary style. It is likely too that his taking refuge in France at the beginning of 1792, when he saw that the court-martial was hopeless, may have been inspired by his new Radical friends. But, after all, France was the most natural refuge for him. England and France were still at peace. And Cobbett, instead of making for Paris, settled down quietly in the village of Tilques, near St. Omer, and set to work perfecting his knowledge of the French language. In August 1792, after nearly six months in France, he set out at length for Paris. But on the way, he heard of the attack on the Tuileries and realised the imminence of war between France and England. At once, he turned round, and made for the coast. His own country was closed to him. He set sail for the United States.

There is, then, no evidence that Cobbett, up to the time of his starting for America, had any political convictions at all. His carrying a letter of introduction from Short, the American *chargé d'affaires*, to Jefferson, appears to show that he had some Radical connections, probably through his associates in issuing *The Soldier's Friend*. But these must have been quite superficial; for there is no sign that he took any part at all in politics after his arrival in America until he was roused by Dr. Priestley's reception. He applied, indeed, to Jefferson, in the hope of getting an administrative post. But when Jefferson said that he had nothing to offer, Cobbett settled down, first at Wilmington and then at Philadelphia, as a teacher of English, chiefly to the French *émigrés* who were then flocking to the United States. Doubtless, he held many discussions on politics with these pupils, who were mostly moderate revolutionaries who had supported the Revolution in its earlier stages. He describes, in the *Life and Adventures*, how one such dispute finally led him into pamphleteering. Doubtless, too, he resented soon the prevailing anti-British sentiment of the Democratic circles to which he had been first introduced. But it is clear that his taking up the political cudgels was a reaction from his surroundings, made the more keen by the contrast with the "loyalist" environment of New Brunswick, rather than any developed or reasoned conviction of political right and wrong. Thomas Carlyle once called Cobbett "the pattern John Bull of his century." Clearly this John Bullishness of his was immensely stimulated by his American experience. He felt himself a lonely John Bull in the American china-shop, and proceeded to break things.

Thus it was that Cobbett boxed the compass of political opinions, while remaining throughout perfectly himself. "Strong as the rhinoceros, and with singular humanities and genialities shining through his thick skin," Carlyle went on to say. "A strong, hale, stout man, with a ruddy countenance, a small laughing eye, and the figure of a respectable farmer," John Silk Buckingham wrote of him in his old age; but the description will do for him at any stage. Egoistic as men are made, but always genial and human. A self-made man inordinately proud of his maker, but without a trace of "swank" or superiority. Violent in controversy, but with a singular instinctive rightness on the great issues. Above all, a great figure among men, because he was one in nature and sentiment with the mass which he aspired to lead. He found his political feet slowly; only when he had seen England and the English people as they were in the early years of the new century did he discover his true faith and allegiance. But he found himself, as a controversialist, without equal, from the very moment when he began to write.

I have chosen the following pieces, from among his voluminous American writings, as the most personal. Some of his other pamphlets, the scurrilous *Life of Thomas Paine*, the *Gros Mousqueton Diplomatique*, or *A Bone to Gnaw for the Democrats*, are every whit as pungent. Some other articles, such as the scandalous abuse of Dr. Rush, are fully as amusing. But none of these, apart from their being fuller of allusions to American politics and politicians of the time, are quite so personal or self-revealing as the pieces I have chosen. And, as one reads Cobbett nowadays for the sake of Cobbett more than of the things or persons of which he writes, this seems the right principle of selection. The reader who wants more can easily get hold of the twelve volumes of *Porcupine's Works* (London, 1801), which, thanks to Cobbett's popularity, is still by no means a scarce book.

That I have enjoyed making this selection is, I hope, obvious. For Cobbett is, above all, a writer to be enjoyed. We have, in English, few enough modern masters of spirited invective. Our controversialists are apt to be as gentlemanly, and as ineffective, as the cartoons in *Punch*. To-day, I suppose a Cobbett would be impossible; his goods would be speedily confiscated for civil, and his person imprisoned for criminal libel, if, indeed, which is unlikely, his printer ever agreed to print his articles. This latter-day politeness is hailed as one of the triumphs of civilisation over barbarism; but I take leave to doubt if the convention that has banished Cobbettism is an unmixed advantage. For there is something to be said for calling a spade a spade, or even more than a spade. And, however successful our civilisation has been in abolishing Cobbetts, it has certainly not abolished spades. A man may begin by wearing gloves for fear of touching the unclean thing; let him beware lest, after long wearing, he forget, or pretend to forget, that the thing is unclean. Cobbett wore no gloves; in his life he touched a great deal of pitch; but I think he was not defiled.

Oxford, April 1927.   G. D. H. COLE.

THE

LIFE AND ADVENTURES

OF

PETER PORCUPINE

———

WITH A FULL AND FAIR ACCOUNT

OF

ALL HIS AUTHORING TRANSACTIONS;

———

BEING A SURE AND INFALLIBLE GUIDE FOR ALL
ENTERPRISING YOUNG MEN WHO WISH TO MAKE
A FORTUNE BY

WRITING PAMPHLETS

———

" Now, you lying varlets, you shall see how a plain tale
will put you down."

SHAKESPEARE.

THE PREFACE

THE celebrated Dean of St. Patrick's somewhere observes that a man of talents no sooner emerges from obscurity, than all the blockheads are instantly up in arms against him. Fully persuaded of the truth of this observation, I should have been prepared for hostility, had I imagined myself a man of talents; but, knowing the contrary too well, I little expected that the harmless essays from my pen would have conjured up against me this numerous and stupid host. It is their misfortune, never to form a right conception of any person or thing, and therefore their abuse is not always a certain proof of merit in the object on which it is bestowed: their ignorance lessens the honour conferred by their envy, hatred and malice.

I have long been the butt of the silly aspersions of this grovelling tribe; but their spite never discovered itself in its deepest colours, till they saw me, as they imagined, " issue from poverty to the " appearance of better condition." Then it was that their gall ran over, and jaundiced their whole countenances; then it was that the stupidest of all stupid gazettes, that lewd and common strumpet, the *Aurora*, became pregnant with the following *bastard*, as abundant in falsehood as any one that ever sprang from the loins of *Poor Richard*.

"*FOR THE AURORA.*

===

"HISTORY OF
"PETER PORCUPINE.

===

" MR. BACHE,

" As the people of America may not be informed
" who PETER PORCUPINE is, the celebrated manu-
" facturer of *lies,* and retailer of *filth,* I will give you
" some little account of this pestiferous animal.
" This wretch was obliged to *abscond* from his dar-
" ling *Old England* to avoid being turned off into
" the other world before, what he supposed, his
" time. It may be well imagined, that in a land
" of liberty, and flowing with milk and honey,
" his *precipitate retreat* could not have been owing
" to any offence committed against the govern-
" ment very honourable to himself. Gnawed by
" the worm that never dies, his own wretchedness
" would ever prevent him from making any at-
" tempt in favour of human happiness. His usual
" occupation at home was that of a *garret-scribbler,*
" excepting a little *night-business* occasionally, to
" supply unavoidable exigencies : Grub-street did
" not answer his purposes, and being scented by
" certain tip-staffs for something more than scrib-
" bling, he took a *French leave* for France. His evil

" genius pursued him here, and *as his fingers were as*
" *long as ever*, he was obliged as suddenly to leave
" the Republic, which has now drawn forth all his
" venom for her attempt to do him *justice*. On his
" arrival in this country, he figured some time as a
" *pedagogue*; but as this employment scarcely fur-
" nished him salt to his porridge, he having been
" literally without hardly bread to eat, and not a
" second shirt to his back, he resumed his old
" occupation of scribbling, having little chance of
" success in the other employments which drove
" him to this country. His talent at *lies* and *Bil-*
" *lingsgate rhetoric*, introduced him to the notice of
" a certain foreign agent, who was known during
" the Revolution by the name of *traitor*. This said
" agent has been seen to pay frequent visits to
" PETER. To atone for his transgressions in the
" mother country, as well as to get a little more
" bread to eat than he had been accustomed to, he
" enlisted in the cause of his gracious majesty.
" From the extreme of poverty and filth, he has
" suddenly sprouted into at least the appearance
" of better condition; for he has taken a house for
" the sale of his large poison, at the enormous rent
" of *twelve hundred dollars a year*, and has *paid a year's*
" *rent in advance ! !* The public will now be enabled
" to account for the overflowings of his gall against
" the Republic of France, and all the Republicans
" of this country, as well as his devotion to the
" cause of tyranny and of Kings. From the fre-
" quency of visits paid him by the agent already
" mentioned, and his sudden change of condition,

" *secret service-money* must have been liberally em-
" ployed; for his zeal to make atonement to his
" mother country seems proportioned to the mag-
" nitude of his offence, and the *guineas* advanced.
" As this *fugitive felon* has crept from his hole, his
" *quills* will now become harmless; for hitherto they
" have only excited apprehension, because the
" beast who shot them was concealed. I have a
" number of anecdotes respecting him, that I will
" soon trouble you with, for the amusement of the
" public. This statement will convince PETER,
" that I know him well, and that I have only dis-
" closed a part of the truth."

" PAUL HEDGEHOG."

This *Paul Hedgehog* I know nothing of. I can
hardly suppose that he is one of my cousins at
New-York: if he be, for the honour of our family,
I hope that he is a bastard. But, let Paul be what
he will, he is not the only one who has attempted
to sink me in the opinion of a public that has ever
honoured my essays with distinguished marks of
approbation. I have been well informed, that it
is currently reported, that Mr. Thomas Bradford,
the bookseller, " put a coat upon my back," and
that, when I was first favoured with his patronage,
I had not a " second shirt to my back."

Were I to calculate upon the usual operations of
truth and gratitude, I should look upon it as impossible that insinuations of this kind had ever been
thrown out by Mr. Bradford, or any of his family;
but, now-a-days, in this happy age of reason and

liberty, we see such extraordinary things happen in the world, that to doubt, at least, does not argue an excess of credulity or incredulity.

Let the propagators of all these falsehoods be who they may, I am much obliged to them for giving me this opportunity of publishing the History of my Life and Adventures, a thing that I was determined to do, whenever a fair occasion offered, and which never could have been so well timed as at the moment when I am stepping into a situation where I may probably continue for the rest of my life.

I here remember well what I said in my *Observations on the Emigration of Dr. Priestley.* " No man " has a right to pry into his neighbour's private " concerns; and the opinions of every man are his " private concerns, while he keeps them so; that " is to say, while they are confined to himself, his " family, and particular friends; but, when he " makes those opinions public; when he once at- " tempts to make converts, whether it be in re- " ligion, politics, or any thing else; when he once " comes forward as a candidate for public admira- " tion, esteem, or compassion, his opinions, his prin- " ciples, his motives, every action of his life, public " or private, become the fair subject of public dis- " cussion."

This is a principle I laid down in the first original page I ever wrote for the press. On this principle it is, that I think myself justified in the present publication, and that I am ready to approve of others for publishing whatever they may know concerning me. Let them write on, till their old pens are worn to the stump: let the devils sweat; let them fire their balls at my reputation, till the very press cries out murder. If ever they hear me whine or complain, I will give them leave to fritter my carcass, and trail my guts along the street, as the French sans-culottes did those of Thomas Mauduit.

THE

LIFE AND ADVENTURES

OF

PETER PORCUPINE

To be descended from an illustrious family certainly reflects honour on any man, in spite of the
sans-culotte principles of the present day. This is,
however, an honour that I have no pretension to.
All that I can boast of in my birth, is, that I was
born in Old England; the country from whence
came the men who explored and settled North
America; the country of Penn, and of all those to
whom this country is indebted.

With respect to my ancestors, I shall go no further back than my grandfather, and for this plain
reason, that I never heard talk of any prior to him.
He was a day-labourer; and I have heard my
father say, that he worked for one farmer from the
day of his marriage to that of his death, upwards
of forty years. He died before I was born, but I
have often slept beneath the same roof that had

sheltered him, and where his widow dwelt for several years after his death. It was a little thatched
cottage, with a garden before the door. It had
but two windows; a damson tree shaded one, and a
clump of filberts the other. Here I and my brothers went every Christmas and Whitsuntide to
spend a week or two, and torment the poor old
woman with our noise and dilapidations. She used
to give us milk and bread for breakfast, an apple
pudding for our dinner, and a piece of bread and
cheese for supper. Her fire was made of turf, cut
from the neighbouring heath, and her evening
light was a rush dipped in grease.

How much better is it, thus to tell the naked
truth, than to descend to such miserable shifts as
Doctor Franklin has had recourse to, in order to
persuade people that his forefathers were men of
wealth and consideration. Not being able to refer
his reader to the herald's office for proofs of the
fame and antiquity of his family, he appeals to the
etymology of his name, and points out a passage in
an obsolete book, whence he has the conscience to
insist on our concluding, that, in the Old English
language, a *Franklin* meant a man of *good reputation and of consequence.* According to Dr. Johnson,
a Franklin was what we now call a gentleman's
steward or land-bailiff, a personage one degree
above a bumbailiff, and that's all.

Every one will, I hope, have the goodness to believe, that my grandfather was no philosopher. Indeed he was not. He never made a lightning-rod,
nor bottled up a single quart of sun-shine, in the

whole course of his life. He was no almanack-maker, nor quack, nor chimney-doctor, nor soap-boiler, nor ambassador, nor printer's devil: neither was he a deist, and all his children were born in wedlock. The legacies he left, were, his scythe, his reap-hook, and his flail; he bequeathed no old and irrecoverable debts to an hospital: he never *cheated the poor during his life*, nor *mocked them in his death*. He has, it is true, been suffered to sleep quietly beneath the green sord; but, if his descendants cannot point to his statue over the door of a library, they have not the mortification to hear him daily accused of having been a whore-master, a hypocrite, and an infidel.

My father, when I was born, was a farmer. The reader will easily believe, from the poverty of his parents, that he had received no very brilliant education: he was, however, learned, for a man in his rank of life. When a little boy, he drove plough for two pence a-day; and these his earnings, were appropriated to the expenses of an evening school. What a village school-master could be expected to teach, he had learnt; and had, besides, considerably improved himself, in several branches of the mathematics. He understood land-surveying well, and was often chosen to draw the plans of disputed territory: in short, he had the reputation of possessing experience and understanding, which never fails, in England, to give a man in a country place, some little weight with his neighbours. He was honest, industrious, and frugal; it was not, therefore, wonderful, that he should be situated in a good farm, and happy in a wife of his own rank, like him, beloved and respected.

So much for my ancestors, from whom, if I derive no honour, I derive no shame.

I had (and I hope I yet have) three brothers: the eldest is a shopkeeper; the second a farmer, and the youngest, if alive, is in the service of the Honourable East India Company, a private soldier, perhaps, as I have been in the service of the king. I was born on the ninth of March, 1766: the exact age of my brothers, I have forgotten; but I remember having heard my mother say, that there was but three years and three quarters difference between the age of the oldest and that of the youngest.

A father like ours, it will be readily supposed, did not suffer us to eat the bread of idleness. I do not remember the time, when I did not earn my living. My first occupation was, driving the small birds from the turnip-seed, and the rooks from the peas. When I first trudged a-field, with my wooden bottle and my satchel swung over my shoulders, I was hardly able to climb the gates and stiles; and, at the close of the day, to reach home, was a task of infinite difficulty. My next employment was weeding wheat, and leading a single horse at harrowing barley. Hoeing peas followed, and hence, I arrived at the honour of joining the reapers in harvest, driving the team, and holding plough. We were all of us strong and laborious, and my father used to boast, that he had four boys, the eldest of whom was but fifteen years old, who

did as much work as any three men in the parish
of Farnham. Honest pride, and happy days!

I have some faint recollection of going to school
to an old woman, who, I believe, did not succeed
in learning me my letters. In the winter evenings,
my father learnt us all to read and write, and gave
us a pretty tolerable knowledge of arithmetic.
Grammar he did not perfectly understand himself, and therefore his endeavours to learn us that,
necessarily failed; for, though he thought he understood it, and though he made us get the rules
by heart, we learnt nothing at all of the principles.

Our religion was that of the Church of England,
to which I have ever remained attached; the more
so, perhaps, as it bears the name of my country.
As my ancestors were never persecuted for their
religious opinions, they never had an opportunity
of giving such a singular proof of their faith, as
Doctor Franklin's grandfather did, when he kept
his Bible under the lid of a close-stool. (What a
book-case!) If I had been in the place of Doctor
Franklin, I never would have related this ridiculous circumstance, especially as it must be construed into a boast of his grandfather's having an
extraordinary degree of veneration for a book,
which, it is well known, he himself *durst* not believe in.

As to politics, we were like the rest of the country
people in England; that is to say, we neither knew
nor thought any thing about the matter. The
shouts of victory, or the murmurs at a defeat,
would now-and-then break in upon our tranquil-

lity for a moment; but I do not remember ever having seen a newspaper in the house; and, most certainly, that privation did not render us less industrious, happy, or free.

After, however, the American war had continued for some time, and the cause and nature of it began to be understood, or rather misunderstood, by the lower classes of the people in England, we became a little better acquainted with subjects of this kind. It is well known, that the people were, as to numbers, nearly equally divided in their opinions, concerning that war, and their wishes respecting the result of it. My father was a partizan of the Americans: he used frequently to dispute on the subject, with the gardener of a nobleman who lived near us. This was generally done with good humour, over a pot of our best ale; yet the disputants sometimes grew warm, and gave way to language that could not fail to attract our attention. My father was worsted, without doubt, as he had for antagonist, a shrewd and sensible old Scotchman, far his superior in political knowledge; but he pleaded before a partial audience: we thought there was but one wise man in the world, and that that one was our father. He who pleaded the cause of the Americans, had an advantage, too, with young minds: he had only to represent the king's troops as sent to cut the throats of a people, our friends and relations, merely because they would not submit to oppression; and his cause was gained. Speaking to the passions, is ever sure to succeed on the uninformed.

Men of integrity are generally pretty obstinate, in adhering to an opinion once adopted. Whether it was owing to this, or to the weakness of Mr. Martin's arguments, I will not pretend to say; but he never could make a convert of my father: he continued an American, and so staunch a one, that he would not have suffered his best friend to drink success to the king's arms at his table. I cannot give the reader a better idea of his obstinacy in this respect, and of the length to which this difference in sentiment was carried in England, than by relating the following instance.

My father used to take one of us with him every year, to the great hop-fair at Wey-Hill. The fair was held at Old Michaelmas-tide, and the journey was, to us, a sort of reward for the labours of the summer. It happened to be my turn to go thither, the very year that Long-Island was taken by the British. A great company of hop-merchants and farmers were just sitting down to supper as the post arrived, bringing in the Extraordinary Gazette, which announced the victory. A hop-factor from London took the paper, placed his chair upon the table, and began to read with an audible voice. He was opposed, a dispute ensued, and my father retired, taking me by the hand, to another apartment, where we supped with about a dozen others of the same sentiments. Here Washington's health, and success to the Americans, were repeatedly toasted, and this was the first time, as far as I can recollect, that I ever heard the General's name mentioned. Little did I then dream, that I should

ever see the man, and still less, that I should hear
some of his own countrymen reviling and execrat-
ing him.

Let not the reader imagine, that I wish to assume
any merit from this mistaken prejudice of an honoured and beloved parent. Whether he was right
or wrong, is not now worth talking about: that I
had no opinion of my own is certain; for, had my
father been on the other side, I should have been
on the other side too; and should have looked upon
the company I then made a part of as malcontents
and rebels. I mention these circumstances, merely
to show that I was not " nursed in the lap of aris-
" tocracy," and that I did not imbibe my principles, or prejudices, from those who were the advocates of blind submission. If my father had any
fault, it was not being submissive enough, and I
am much afraid, my acquaintance have but too
often discovered the same fault in his son.

It would be as useless as unentertaining, to dwell
on the occupations and sports of a country boy;
to lead the reader to fairs, cricket-matches, and
hare-hunts. I shall therefore come at once to the
epoch, when an accident happened, that gave that
turn to my future life, which at last brought me to
the United States.

Towards the autumn of 1782, I went to visit a
relation who lived in the neighbourhood of Portsmouth. From the top of Portsdown, I, for the first
time, beheld the sea, and no sooner did I behold
it, than I wished to be a sailor. I could never account for this sudden impulse, nor can I now.

Almost all English boys feel the same inclination:
it would seem that, like young ducks, instinct leads
them to rush on the bosom of the water.

But it was not the sea alone that I saw: the
grand fleet was riding at anchor at Spithead. I
had heard of the wooden walls of Old England: I
had formed my ideas of a ship, and of a fleet; but,
what I now beheld, so far surpassed what I had
ever been able to form a conception of, that I stood
lost between astonishment and admiration. I had
heard talk of the glorious deeds of our admirals
and sailors, of the defeat of the Spanish Armada,
and of all those memorable combats, that good
and true Englishmen never fail to relate to their
children about a hundred times a year. The brave
Rodney's victories over our natural enemies, the
French and Spaniards, had long been the theme
of our praise, and the burden of our songs. The
sight of the fleet brought all these into my mind;
in confused order, it is true, but with irresistible
force. My heart was inflated with national pride.
The sailors were my countrymen; the fleet be-
longed to my country, and surely I had my part in
it, and in all its honours; yet, these honours I had
not earned; I took to myself a sort of reproach, for
possessing what I had no right to, and resolved to
have a just claim by sharing in the hardships and
dangers.

I arrived at my uncle's late in the evening, with
my mind full of my sea-faring project. Though I
had walked thirty miles during the day, and consequently was well wearied, I slept not a moment.

It was no sooner day-light, than I arose and walked down towards the old castle, on the beach of Spithead. For a sixpence given to an invalid, I got permission to go upon the battlements; here I had a closer view of the fleet, and at every look my impatience to be on board increased. In short, I went from the castle to Portsmouth, got into a boat, and was in a few minutes on board the Pegasus man of war.

The Captain had more compassion than is generally met with in men of his profession: he represented to me the toils I must undergo, and the punishment that the least disobedience or neglect would subject me to. He persuaded me to return home, and I remember he concluded his advice, with telling me, that it was better to be led to church in a halter, to be tied to a girl that I did not like, than to be tied to the gang-way, or, as the sailors call it, married to *miss roper*. From the conclusion of this wholesome counsel, I perceived that the Captain thought I had eloped on account of a bastard. I blushed, and that confirmed him in his opinion; but I declare to the reader, that I was no more guilty of such an offence, than Mr. Swanwick, or any other gentleman who is constitutionally virtuous. No; thank heaven, I have none of the Franklintonian crimes to accuse myself of; my children do not hang their hats up in other men's houses; I am neither patriot nor philosopher.

I in vain attempted to convince Captain Berkley, that choice alone had led me to the sea; he sent me on shore, and I at last quitted Portsmouth;

but not before I had applied to the Port-Admiral, Evans, to get my name enrolled among those who were destined for the service. I was, in some sort, obliged to acquaint the Admiral with what had passed on board the Pegasus, in consequence of which, my request was refused, and I happily escaped, sorely against my will, from the most toilsome and perilous profession in the world.

I returned once more to the plough, but I was spoiled for a farmer. I had, before my Portsmouth adventure, never known any other ambition than that of surpassing my brothers in the different labours of the field; but it was quite otherwise now; I sighed for a sight of the world; the little island of Britain, seemed too small a compass for me. The things in which I had taken the most delight were neglected; the singing of the birds grew insipid, and even the heart-cheering cry of the hounds, after which I formerly used to fly from my work, bound o'er the fields, and dash through the brakes and coppices, was heard with the most torpid indifference. Still, however, I remained at home till the following spring, when I quitted it, perhaps, for ever.

It was on the sixth of May 1783, that I, like Don Quixote, sallied forth to seek adventures. I was dressed in my holiday clothes, in order to accompany two or three lasses to Guildford fair. They were to assemble at a house, about three miles from my home, where I was to attend them; but, unfortunately for me, I had to cross the London turnpike road. The stage-coach had just turned

the summit of a hill, and was rattling down towards me at a merry rate. The notion of going to
London, never entered my mind, till this very moment, yet the step was completely determined on,
before the coach came to the spot where I stood.
Up I got, and was in London about nine o'clock
in the evening.

It was by mere accident, that I had money
enough to defray the expenses of this day. Being
rigged out for the fair, I had three or four crown
and half-crown pieces, (which most certainly I did
not intend to spend), besides a few shillings and
half-pence. This, my little all, which I had been
years in amassing, melted away, like snow before
the sun, when touched by the fingers of the inn-
keepers and their waiters. In short, when I arrived at Ludgate-Hill, and had paid my fare, I
had but about half a crown in my pocket.

By a commencement of that good luck, which
has hitherto attended me, through all the situa-
tions in which fortune has placed me, I was preserved from ruin. A gentleman, who was one of
the passengers in the stage, fell into conversation
with me at dinner, and he soon learnt that I was
going, I knew not whither, nor for what. This
gentleman was a hop-merchant in the borough of
Southwark, and, upon closer inquiry, it appeared
that he had often dealt with my father at Wey-
Hill. He knew the danger I was in; he was himself a father, and he felt for my parents. His house
became my home; he wrote to my father, and endeavoured to prevail on me to obey his orders,

which were to return immediately home. I am ashamed to say that I was disobedient. It was the first time I had ever been so, and I have repented of it from that moment to this. Willingly would I have returned; but pride would not suffer me to do it. I feared the scoffs of my acquaintances more than the real evils that threatened me.

My generous preserver, finding my obstinacy not to be overcome, began to look out for an employment for me. He was preparing an advertisement for the newspaper, when an acquaintance of his, an attorney, called in to see him. He related my adventure to this gentleman, whose name was Holland, and who, happening to want an understrapping quill-driver, did me the honour to take me into his service, and the next day saw me perched upon a great high stool, in an obscure chamber in Gray's Inn, endeavouring to decipher the crabbed draughts of my employer.

I could write a good plain hand, but I could not read the pot-hooks and hangers of Mr. Holland. He was a month in learning me to copy without almost continual assistance, and even then I was of but little use to him; for, besides that I wrote a snail's pace, my want of knowledge in orthography, gave him infinite trouble: so that, for the first two months, I was a dead weight upon his hands. Time, however, rendered me useful; and Mr. Holland was pleased to tell me, that he was very well satisfied with me, just at the very moment when I began to grow extremely dissatisfied with him,

No part of my life has been totally unattended with pleasure, except the eight or nine months I passed in Gray's Inn. The office (for so the dungeon where I wrote was called) was so dark, that, on cloudy days, we were obliged to burn candle. I worked like a galley-slave from five in the morning till eight or nine at night, and sometimes all night long. How many quarrels have I assisted to foment and perpetuate between those poor innocent fellows, John Doe and Richard Roe! How many times (God forgive me!) have I sent them to assault each other with guns, swords, staves and pitchforks, and then brought them to answer for their misdeeds before our Sovereign Lord the King seated in His Court of Westminster! When I think of the *saids* and *soforths*, and the counts of tautology that I scribbled over; when I think of those sheets of seventy-two words, and those lines two inches apart, my brain turns. Gracious heaven! if I am doomed to be wretched, bury me beneath Iceland snows, and let me feed on blubber; stretch me under the burning line, and deny me thy propitious dews; nay, if it be thy will, suffocate me with the infected and pestilential air of a democratic club-room; but save me from the desk of an attorney!

Mr. Holland was but little in the chambers himself. He always went out to dinner, while I was left to be provided for by the *laundress*, as he called her. Those gentlemen of the law, who have resided in the Inns of Court in London, know very well what a *laundress* means. Ours was, I believe, the oldest and ugliest of the sisterhood. She had age and experience enough to be Lady Abbess of all the nuns in all the convents of Irish-Town. It would be wronging the witch of Endor to compare her to this hag, who was the only creature that deigned to enter into conversation with me. All except the name, I was in prison, and this weird sister was my keeper. Our chambers were, to me, what the subterraneous cavern was to Gil Blas: his description of the Dame Leonarda exactly suited my laundress; nor were the professions, or rather the practice, of our masters altogether dissimilar.

I never quitted this gloomy recess except on Sundays, when I usually took a walk to St. James's Park, to feast my eyes with the sight of the trees, the grass, and the water. In one of these walks I happened to cast my eye on an advertisement, inviting all loyal young men, who had a mind to gain riches and glory, to repair to a certain rendezvous, where they might enter into His Majesty's marine service, and have the peculiar happiness and honour of being enrolled in the Chatham Division. I was not ignorant enough to be the dupe of this morsel of military bombast; but a change was what I wanted: besides, I knew that marines went to sea, and my desire to be on that element had rather increased than diminished by my being penned up in London. In short, I resolved to join this glorious corps; and, to avoid all possibility of being discovered by my friends, I went down to Chatham and enlisted, into the marines as I thought, but the next morning I found myself before a Captain of a marching regiment. There was no retreating: I had taken a shilling to drink his Majesty's health, and his further bounty was ready for my reception.

When I told the Captain (who was an Irishman, and who has since been an excellent friend to me), that I thought myself engaged in the marines: " By Jasus! my lad," said he, " and you have had " a narrow escape." He told me, that the regiment into which I had been so happy as to enlist, was one of the oldest and boldest in the whole army, and that it was at that moment serving in that fine, flourishing, and plentiful country, Nova Scotia. He dwelt long on the beauties and riches of this terrestrial paradise, and dismissed me, perfectly enchanted with the prospect of a voyage thither.

I enlisted early in 1784, and, as peace had then taken place, no great haste was made to send recruits off to their regiments. I remained upwards of a year at Chatham, during which time I was employed in learning my exercise, and taking my tour in the duty of the garrison. My leisure time, which was a very considerable portion of the twenty-four hours, was spent, not in the dissipations common to such a way of life, but in reading and study. In the course of this year I learnt more than I had ever done before. I subscribed to a circulating library at Brompton, the greatest part of the books in which I read more than once over. The library was not very considerable, it is true, nor in my reading was I directed by any degree of taste or choice. Novels, plays, history, poetry, all were read, and nearly with equal avidity.

Such a course of reading could be attended with but little profit: it was skimming over the surface of everything. One branch of learning, however, I went to the bottom with, and that the most essential branch too, the grammar of my mother tongue. I had experienced the want of a knowledge of grammar during my stay with Mr. Holland; but it is very probable that I never should have thought of encountering the study of it, had not accident placed me under a man whose friendship extended beyond his interest. Writing a fair hand procured me the honour of being copyist to Colonel Debeig, the commandant of the garrison. I transcribed the famous correspondence between him and the Duke of Richmond, which ended in the good and gallant old Colonel being stripped of the reward, bestowed on him for his long and meritorious servitude.

Being totally ignorant of the rules of grammar, I necessarily made many mistakes in copying, because no one can copy letter by letter, nor even word by word. The Colonel saw my deficiency, and strongly recommended study. He enforced his advice with a sort of injunction, and with a promise of reward in case of success.

I procured me a Lowth's grammar, and applied myself to the study of it with unceasing assiduity, and not without some profit; for, though it was a considerable time before I fully comprehended all that I read, still I read and studied with such unremitted attention, that, at last, I could write without falling into any very gross errors. The pains I took cannot be described: I wrote the whole grammar out two or three times; I got it by heart; I repeated it every morning and every evening, and, when on guard, I imposed on myself the task of saying it all over once every time I was posted sentinel. To this exercise of my memory I ascribe the retentiveness of which I have since found it capable, and to the success with which it was attended, I ascribe the perseverance that has led to the acquirement of the little learning of which I am master.

This study was, too, attended with another advantage: it kept me out of mischief. I was always sober, and regular in my attendance; and, not being a clumsy fellow, I met with none of those reproofs, which disgust so many young men with the service.

There is no situation where merit is so sure to meet with reward as in a well-disciplined army. Those who command are obliged to reward it for their own ease and credit. I was soon raised to the rank of corporal; a rank, which, however contemptible it may appear in some people's eyes, brought me in a clear twopence *per diem*, and put a very clever worsted knot upon my shoulder too. Don't you laugh now, Mr. Swanwick; a worsted knot is a much more honourable mark of distinction than a *custom-house badge*; though, I confess, the king must have such people as tide-waiters as well as corporals.

As promotion began to dawn, I grew impatient to get to my regiment, where I expected soon to bask under the rays of royal favour. The happy day of departure at last came: we set sail from Gravesend, and, after a short and pleasant passage, arrived at Halifax in Nova Scotia. When I first beheld the barren, not to say hideous, rocks at the entrance of the harbour, I began to fear that the master of the vessel had mistaken his way; for I could perceive nothing of that fertility that my good recruiting Captain had dwelt on with so much delight.

Nova Scotia had no other charm for me than that of novelty. Every thing I saw was new: bogs, rocks and stumps, musquitoes and bull-frogs. Thousands of captains and colonels without soldiers, and of squires without stockings or shoes. In England, I had never thought of approaching a squire without a most respectful bow: but, in this new world, though I was but a corporal, I often ordered a squire to bring me a glass of grog, and even to take care of my knapsack.

We staid but a few weeks in Nova Scotia, being ordered to St. John's, in the province of New Brunswick. Here, and at other places in the same province, we remained till the month of September, 1791, when the regiment was relieved and sent home.

We landed at Portsmouth on the 3d of November, and on the 19th of the next month I obtained my discharge, after having served not quite eight years, and after having, in that short space, passed

through every rank, from that of a private sentinel
to that of serjeant major, without ever being once
disgraced, confined, or even reprimanded.—But
let my superiors speak for me, they will tell my
friends and all my readers what I was during my
servitude.

" *By the Right Honourable Major Lord Edward Fitz-*
" *gerald, commanding his Majesty's 54th Regiment*
" *of Foot, whereof Lieutenant General Frederick is*
" *Colonel.*

" THESE are to certify, that the bearer hereof,
" WILLIAM COBBETT, Serjeant Major in the afore-
" said regiment, has served honestly and faithfully
" for the space of eight years, nearly seven of which
" he has been a non-commissioned officer, and of
" that time he has been five years Serjeant Major
" to the regiment; but having very earnestly ap-
" plied for his discharge, he, in consideration of
" his good behaviour, and the services he has ren-
" dered the regiment, is hereby discharged.

" Given under my hand and the seal of the
" regiment, at Portsmouth, this 19th day
" of December, 1791.
" EDWARD FITZGERALD."

I shall here add the orders, issued in the garrison
of Portsmouth on the day of my discharge.

" Portsmouth, 19th Dec. 1791.
" Serjeant Major Cobbett having most press-
" ingly applied for his discharge, at Major Lord
" Edward Fitzgerald's request, General Frederick

" has granted it. General Frederick has ordered
" Major Lord Edward Fitzgerald to return the
" Serjeant Major thanks for his behaviour and
" conduct during the time of his being in the regi-
" ment, and Major Lord Edward adds his most
" hearty thanks to those of the General."

After having laid these pieces before my reader,
I beg him to recollect what the *Argus* of New-
York, and the *Aurora* of Philadelphia, have asserted concerning Peter Porcupine's being flogged
in his regiment for thieving, and afterwards de-
serting. The monstrous, disorganizing, democratic
gang were not aware that I was in possession of
such uncontrovertible proofs as these.

I hope, I may presume that my character will be
looked upon as good, down to the date of my discharge; and, if so, it only remains for me to give
an account of myself from that time to this.

The Democrats have asserted, as may be seen
in the preface, that I got my living in London by
" garret-scribbling," and that I was obliged to
take a *French leave* for France, for some " *night*
" *work*."—Now, the fact is, I went to France in
March, 1792, and I landed at New York in the
month of October following; so that, I had but
three months to follow "garret-scribbling" in London. How these three months were employed it
is not necessary to say here, but that I had not
much leisure for " garret-scribbling " the ladies
will be well convinced, when I tell them that I got
a wife in the time. As to the charge concerning

" night work," I am afraid I must plead guilty,
but not with my " fingers," as these malicious fellows would insinuate. No, no, I am no relation to
Citizen *Plato*: the French ladies do not call me,
the *garçon fendu.*

Before I go any further, it seems necessary to say
a word or two about " French leave." Did this
expression escape the Democrats in an unwary
moment? Why " French leave"? Do they wish to
insinuate, that nobody but *Frenchmen* are obliged
to fly from the hands of thief-catchers? The Ger-
mans, and after them the English, have applied
this degrading expression to the French nation;
but, is it not inconsistent, and even ungrateful, for
those who are in the interest, and perhaps, in the
pay, of that magnanimous republic, to talk about
"French leave"? It is something curious that
this expression should find a place in a paragraph
wherein I am accused of abusing the French. The
fact is, the friendship professed by these people,
towards the French nation, is all grimace, all hypocrisy : the moment they are off their guard, they
let us see that it is the abominable system of French
tyranny that they are attached to, and not to the
people of that country.—" French leave! " The
leave of a *runaway*, a *thief*, a *Tom Paine!* What
could the most prejudiced, the bitterest Englishman have said more galling and severe against the
whole French nation? They cry out against me
for " *abusing* " the cut-throats of Nantz and other
places, and for accusing the demagogue-tyrants of
robbery ; while they themselves treat the whole

nation as thieves. This is the democratic way of washing out stains; just as the sweet and cleanly Sheelah washes her gentle Dermot's face with a dishclout.

Leaving the ingenious citizens to extricate themselves from this hobble, or fall under the displeasure of their masters, I shall return to my adventures.—I arrived in France in March, 1792, and continued there till the beginning of September following, the six happiest months of my life. I should be the most ungrateful monster that ever existed, were I to speak ill of the French people in general. I went to that country full of all those prejudices, that Englishmen suck in with their mother's milk, against the French and against their religion: a few weeks convinced me that I had been deceived with respect to both. I met everywhere with civility, and even hospitality, in a degree that I never had been accustomed to. I found the people, among whom I lived, excepting those who were already blasted with the principles of the accursed revolution, honest, pious, and kind to excess.

People may say what they please about the misery of the French peasantry, under the old government; I have conversed with thousands of them, not ten among whom did not regret the change. I have not room here to go into an inquiry into the causes that have led these people to become the passive instruments, the slaves of a set of tyrants such as the world never saw before, but I venture to predict, that, sooner or later, they will

return to that form of government under which
they were happy and under which alone they can
ever be so again.

My determination to settle in the United States
was formed before I went to France, and even before I quitted the army. A desire of seeing a country, so long the theatre of a war of which I had
heard and read so much; the flattering picture
given of it by Raynal; and, above all, an inclination for seeing the world, led me to this determination. It would look a little like coaxing for me to
say, that I had imbibed principles of republicanism, and that I was ambitious to become a citizen
of a free state, but this was really the case, I
thought that men enjoyed here a greater degree of
liberty than in England; and this, if not the principal reason, was at least one, for my coming to
this country.

I did intend to stay in France till the spring of
1793, as well to perfect myself in the language,
as to pass the winter at Paris; but I perceived the
storm gathering; I saw that a war with England
was inevitable, and it was not difficult to foresee
what would be the fate of Englishmen, in that
country, where the rulers had laid aside even the
appearance of justice and mercy. I wished, however, to see Paris, and had actually hired a coach
to go thither. I was even on the way, when I
heard, at Abbeville, that the king was dethroned
and his guards murdered. This intelligence made
me turn off towards Havre-de-Grace, whence I
embarked for America.

I beg leave here to remind the reader, that one of the lying paragraphs, lately published in the lying *Aurora*, states, that I was whipped at Paris, and that hence I bear a grudge against the French Republic. Now, I never was at Paris, as I can prove by the receipts for my board and lodging, from the day I entered France to that of my leaving it; and, as to the Republic, as it is called, I could have no grudge against it; for the tyrants had not given it that name, when I was so happy as to bid it an eternal adieu. Had I remained a few months longer I make no doubt that I should have had reason to execrate it as every other man, woman, and child has, who has had the misfortune to groan under its iron anarchy.

Some little time after my arrival in this country, I sent Mr. Jefferson, then Secretary of State, a letter of recommendation, which I had brought from the American Ambassador at the Hague. The following is a copy of the letter Mr. Jefferson wrote me on that occasion.

" Philadelphia, Nov. 5th, 1792.
" Sir,
" In acknowledging the receipt of your favour
" of the 2d instant, I wish it were in my power to
" announce to you any way in which I could be
" useful to you. Mr. Short's assurances of your
" merit would be a sufficient inducement to me.
" Public Offices in our government are so few,
" and of so little value, as to offer no resource to
" talents. When you shall have been here some

" small time, you will be able to judge in what way
" you can set out with the best prospect of suc-
" cess, and if I can serve you in it, I shall be very
" ready to do it.

" I am,

" Sir,

" Your very humble servant,

" TH. JEFFERSON."

I will just observe on this letter, that it was
thankfully received, and that, had I stood in need
of Mr. Jefferson's services, I should have applied
to him; but as that did not appear likely to be the
case, I wrote him a letter some few months afterwards, requesting him to assist a poor man, the
bearer of it, and telling him that I should look
upon the assistance as given to myself. I dare say
he complied with my request, for the person recommended was in deep distress, and a *Frenchman.*

With respect to the authenticity of this letter
there can be no doubt. I have shown the original,
as well as those of the other documents here transcribed, to more than fifty gentlemen of the city of
Philadelphia, and they may, at any time, be seen
by any person of credit, who wishes a sight of
them. Nor have I confined the perusal of them to
those who have the misfortune to be deemed aristocrats. Among persons of distant places, I have
shown them to Mr. *Ketletas* of New York, who, I
must do him the justice to say, had the candour
to express a becoming detestation of the base cut-
throat author of the threatening letter sent to Mr.
Oldden.

I have now brought myself to the United States, and have enabled the reader to judge of me so far. It remains for me to negative two assertions, which apply to my authoring transactions; the one is, that " Mr. Bradford *put a coat upon my back*; " and the other, that I am, or have been, " in the pay of " a British Agent."

In the month of July, 1794, the famous Unitarian Doctor, fellow of the *Royal* Society, London, *citizen* of France, and delegate to the *Grande Convention Nationale* of notorious memory, landed at New-York. His landing was nothing to me, nor to any body else; but, the fulsome and consequential addresses, sent him by the pretended patriots, and his canting replies, at once calculated to flatter the people here, and to degrade his country and mine, was something to me. It was my business, and the business of every man, who thinks that truth ought to be opposed to malice and hypocrisy.

When the *Observatirns* on the emigration of this " martyr to the cause of liberty," were ready for the press, I did not, at first, offer them to Mr. Bradford. I knew him to retain a rooted hatred against Great Britain, and concluded, that his principles would prevent him from being instrumental in the publication of any thing that tended to unveil one of its most bitter enemies. I therefore addressed myself to Mr. Carey. This was, to make use of a culinary figure, jumping out of the frying-pan into the fire. Mr. Carey received me as booksellers generally receive authors (I mean authors

whom they hope to get but little by) : he looked at
the title, from top to bottom, and then at me, from
head to foot.—" No, *my lad*," says he, " I don't
" think it will suit."—*My lad !*—God in heaven
forgive me! I believe that, at that moment, I
wished for another yellow fever to strike the city;
not to destroy the inhabitants, but to furnish me
too, with *the subject of a pamphlet*, that might make
me rich.—Mr. Carey has sold hundreds of the *Observations* since that time, and therefore, I dare say,
he highly approved of them, when he came to a
perusal. At any rate, I must not forget to say, that
he behaved honourably in the business; for, he
promised not to make known the author, and he
certainly kept his word, or the discovery would not
have been reserved for the month of June, 1796.
This circumstance, considering Mr. Carey's politics, is greatly to his honour, and has almost wiped
from my memory, that contumelious " *my lad*."

From Mr. Carey, I went to Mr. Bradford, and
left the pamphlet for his perusal. The next day, I
went to him, to know his determination. He hesitated, wanted to know if I could not make it a
little *more popular*, adding that, unless I could, he
feared that the publishing of it would endanger
his windows. More popular, I could not make it. I
never was of an accommodating disposition in my
life. The only alteration I would consent to, was
in the title. I had given the pamphlet the double
title of "*The Tartuffe Detected*; or, *Observations*,
" &c." The former was suppressed, though, had
I not been pretty certain that every press in the

city was as little free, as that to which I was sending it, the *Tartuffe Detected*, should have remained;
for the person on whom it was bestowed, merited
it much better than the character so named by
Molière.

These difficulties, and these fears of the bookseller, at once opened my eyes with respect to the
boasted liberty of the press. Because the laws of
this country proclaim to the world, that every man
may write and publish freely; and because I saw
the newspapers filled with vaunts on the subject,
I was fool enough to imagine, that the press was
really free for every one. I had not the least idea,
that a man's windows were in danger of being
broken, if he published any thing that was *not
popular*. I did, indeed, see the words *liberty* and
equality; the *rights of man*, the *crimes of kings*, and
such like, in most of the booksellers' windows; but
I did not know that they were put there to save
the glass, as a free republican Frenchman puts a
cockade tricolor in his hat, to save his head. I was
ignorant of all these *arcana* of the liberty of the
press.

If it had so happened, that one of the Whiskey-
Boys had went over to England, and had received
addresses from any part of the people there, con-
gratulating him on his escape, from a nation of
ruffians, and beseeching the Lord, that those ruffians might " tread back the paths of *infamy* and
" *ruin*; " and if this emigrating " *Martyr* " in the
cause of Whiskey, had echoed back the hypocritical
cant; and if he and all his palavering addressers

had been detected and exposed by some good
American in London, would not such an American
have received the applause of all men of virtue
and sense? And what would, or rather what would
not have been said here against the prostituted
press of Great Britain, had an English bookseller
testified his fears to publish the truth, lest his windows should be dashed in?

The work that it was feared would draw down
punishment on the publisher, did not contain one
untruth, one anarchical, indecent, immoral, or ir-
religious expression; and yet the bookseller feared
for his windows! For what? Because it was not
popular enough. A bookseller, in a *despotic* state, fears
to publish a work that is *too popular*; and one in a
free state, fears to publish a work that is not *popular
enough.* I leave it to the learned philosophers of
the " Age of Reason," to determine in which of
these states there is the most liberty of the press;
for, I must acknowledge, the point is too nice for
me: fear is fear, whether inspired by a Sovereign
Lord the King, or by a Sovereign People.

I shall be told, that Mr. Bradford's fears were
groundless. It may be so; but he ought to be a
competent judge of the matter; he must know the
extent of the liberty of the press, better than I
could. He might be mistaken; but that he was
sincere, appeared clearly from his not putting his
name at the bottom of the title page. Even the
Bone to Gnaw for the Democrats, which did not appear till about six months afterwards, was " Pub-
" lished for the Purchasers." It was not till long

after the public had fixed the seal of approbation on these pamphlets, that they were honoured with the bookseller's name. It was something curious, that the second and third, and fourth editions should be entitled to a mark of respect, that the first was not worthy of. Poor little innocents! They were thrown on the parish like foundlings; no soul would own them, till it was found that they possessed the gift of bringing in the pence. Another singularity is, they got into better paper as they advanced. So the prudent matron changes the little dirty ragged wench into a fine mademoiselle, as soon as she perceives that the beaux begin to cast their eyes on her.

But, it is time to return, and give the reader an account of my gains. The pecuniary concerns of an author, are always the most interesting.

The terms on which Mr. Bradford took the *Observations*, were what booksellers call *publishing it together*. I beg the reader, if he foresees the possibility of his becoming author, to recollect this phrase well. *Publishing it together*, is thus managed: the bookseller takes the work, prints it, and defrays all expenses of paper, binding, &c. and the profits, if any, are divided between him and the author. ——Long after the *Observations* were sold off, Mr. Bradford rendered me an account (undoubtedly a very just one) of the sales. According to this account, my share of the profits (my share only) amounted to the sum of *one shilling and seven-pence half-penny*, currency of the state of Pennsylvania, (or, about eleven-pence three farthings sterling)

quite entirely clear of all deductions whatso-
ever!

Now, bulky 'as this sum appears in words at
length, I presume, that when 1s. 7½ is reduced to
figures, no one will suppose it sufficient to put a
coat upon my back. If my poor back were not too
broad to be clothed with such a sum as this, God
knows how I should bear all that has been, and is,
and is to be, laid on it by the unmerciful democrats. Why! 1s. 7½ would not cover the back of a
Lilliputian! no, not even in rags, as they sell here.

Besides, this clothing story will at once fall to
the ground, when I assure the reader (and Mr.
Carey will bear witness to the truth of what I say),
that, when I offered this work for publication, I
had as good a coat upon my back, as ever Mr.
Bradford, or any of his brother booksellers, put on
in their lives; and, what is more, this coat was my
own. No tailor nor shoemaker ever had my name
in his books.

After the *Observations*, Mr. Bradford and I *published it together* no longer. When a pamphlet was
ready for the press, we made a bargain for it, and
I took his note of hand, payable in one, two, or
three months. That the public may know exactly
what gains I have derived from the publications
that issued from Mr. Bradford's, I here subjoin a
list of them, and the sums received in payment.

	Dols.	Cents.
Observations . .	0	21
Bone to Gnaw, 1st Part .	125	0

	Dols.	Cents.
Kick for a Bite . .	20	0
Bone to Gnaw, 2d Part .	40	0
Plain English . .	100	0
New Year's Gift . .	100	0
Prospect . . .	18	0
Total	403	21

The best way of giving the reader an idea of the generosity of my bookseller is, to tell him, that, upon my going into business for myself, I offered to purchase the copy-rights of these pamphlets at the same price that I had sold them at. Mr. Bradford's refusing to sell, is a clear proof that they were worth more than he gave me, even after they had passed through several editions. Let it not be said, then, that he put a coat upon my back.

My concerns with Mr. Bradford, closed with *The Prospect from the Congress Gallery*, and, as our separation has given rise to conjectures and reports, I shall trouble the reader with an explanation of the matter.

I proposed making a mere collection of the debates, with here and there a note, by way of remarks. It was not my intention to publish it in Numbers, but at the end of the session, in one volume; but Mr. Bradford, fearing a want of success in this form, determined on publishing in Numbers. This was without my approbation, as was also a subscription that was opened for the support of the work. When

D

about half a Number was finished, I was informed
that many gentlemen had expressed their desire,
that the work might contain a good deal of original
matter, and few debates. In consequence of this, I
was requested to alter my plan; I said I would, but
that I would by no means undertake to continue the
work.

The first Number, as it was called (but not by
me), was published, and its success led Mr. Bradford to press for a continuation. His son offered me,
I believe, a hundred dollars a Number, in place
of eighteen; and, I should have accepted his offer,
had it not been for a word that escaped him
during the conversation. He observed, that their
customers would be much disappointed; for that,
his *father had promised* a continuation, and *that it
should be made very interesting.* This slip of the tongue,
opened my eyes at once. What! a bookseller undertake to promise that I should write, and that I
should write to please his customers too! No; if
all his *customers,* if all the Congress, with the President at their head, had come and solicited me;
nay, had my life depended on a compliance, I
would not have written another line.

I was fully employed at this time, having a translation on my hands for Mr. Moreau de St. Mery,
as well as another work which took up a great deal
of my time; so that, I believe, I should not have
published the *Censor,* had it not been to convince
the *customers* of Mr. Bradford, that I was not in his
pay; that I was not the puppet, and he the show-
man. That, whatever merits or demerits my

writings might have, no part of them fell to his share.

When Mr. Bradford found I was preparing to publish a continuation of the remarks on the debates, he sent me the following note:

" Sir,

" Send me your account, and a receipt for the " last publication, and your money shall be sent " you by

" Yours, &c.

" Tho. Bradford."

" Phila. April 22, 1796."

To this I returned, for answer:

" Philadelphia, 22d March, 1796.

" Sir,

" I have the honour to possess your laconic note ; " but, upon my word, I do not understand it. The " requesting of a receipt from a person, before any " tender of money is made, and the note being " dated in April, in place of March; these things " throw such an obscurity over the whole, that I " defer complying with its contents, till I have the " pleasure of seeing yourself.

" I am

" Your most obedient

" Humble servant,

" Wm. Cobbett."

This brought me a second note, in these words:

" Sir,

" Finding you mean to pursue the *Prospect*, which
" you sold to me, I now make a demand of the
" *fulfillment* of your contract, and if honour does
" not prompt you to *fulfill* your engagements, you
" may rely on an *applycation* to the laws of my
" country, and make no doubt, I shall there meet
" you on such grounds as will convince you I am
" not to be trifled with.

" I am

" Yours, &c.

" Tho. Bradford."

" March 22, 1796."

Here ended the correspondence, except that it
might be said to be continued for about five minutes longer by the hearty laugh, that I bestowed
on this *correct* and polite billet.

It is something truly singular, that Mr. Bradford should threaten me with a prosecution for not
writing, just at the moment that others threatened
me with a prosecution for writing. It seemed a
little difficult to set both at open defiance, yet this
was done, by continuing to write, and by employ-
ing another bookseller.

Indeed, these booksellers in general, are a cruel
race. They imagine that the soul and body of
every author that falls into their hands, is their
exclusive property. They have adopted the bird-
catcher's maxim: " a bird that can sing, and wont

" sing, ought to be made sing." Whenever their devils are out of employment, the drudging goblin of an author, must sharpen up his pen, and never think of repose, till he is relieved by the arrival of a more profitable job. Then the wretch may remain as undisturbed as a sleep-mouse in winter, while the stupid dolt whom he has clad and fattened, receives the applause.

I now come to the assertion, that I am, or have been, in the pay of the British government.

In the first place, the democrats swear, that I have been " frequently visited by a certain Agent," meaning I suppose, Mr. Bond : to this I answer, that it is an abominable lie. I never saw Mr. Bond but three times in my life, and then I had business with him, as the interpreter of Frenchmen, who wanted certificates from him, in order to secure their property in the conquered colonies. I never in my life spoke to, corresponded with, or even saw, to my knowledge, either of the British Ministers, or any one of their retinue. Mr. Bradford once told me, that Mr. Allen, the father-in-law of Mr. Hammond, said he was acquainted with me. If this gentleman did really say so, he joked; for he never saw me in his life, that I know of.

A little while after the New Year's Gift was published, an attack was made in the *Argus* of New York, on the supposed author of it; in consequence of which, this supposed author, or some one in his behalf, took occasion to observe in Mr. Claypoole's paper, that it was uncandid to attribute to a gentleman of irreproachable character, what was well

known to be the work of a democrat. I had a
great mind to say, at that time, what I shall now
say; and that is, that let this gentleman be who he
will, I think myself as good as he, and of as good
a character too; and that, as to the dishonour attached to the publication, I am willing to take it
all to myself.

It is hard to prove a negative; it is what no man
is expected to do; yet, I think I can prove that the
accusation of my being in British pay, is not supported by one single fact, or the least shadow of
probability.

When a foreign government hires a writer, it
takes care that his labours shall be distributed,
whether the readers are all willing to pay for them
or not. This we daily see verified in the distri-
bution of certain blasphemous gazettes, which,
though kicked from the door with disdain, flies in
at the window.   Now, has this ever been the case
with the works of Peter Porcupine? Were they
ever thrusted upon people in spite of their remon-
strances? Can Mr. Bradford say, that thousands
of these pamphlets have ever been paid for by any
agent of Great Britain? Can he say, that I have
ever distributed any of them? No; he can say no
such thing. They had, at first, to encounter every
difficulty, and they have made their way, supported by public approbation, and by that alone.
Mr. Bradford, if he is candid enough to repeat
what he told me, will say, that the British Consul,
when he purchased half a dozen of them, insisted
upon having them *at the wholesale price !* Did this

look like a desire to encourage them? Besides, those who know anything of Mr. Bradford, will never believe, that he would have lent his aid to a British Agent's publications; for, of all the Americans I have yet conversed with, he seems to entertain the greatest degree of rancour against that nation.

I have every reason to believe, that the British Consul was far from approving of some, at least, of my publications. I happened to be in a bookseller's shop, unseen by him, when he had the goodness to say, that I was a " *wild fellow.*" On which I shall only observe, that when the King bestows on me about five hundred pounds sterling a-year, perhaps, I may become a *tame fellow*, and hear my master, my countrymen, my friends, and my parents, belied and execrated, without saying one single word in their defence.

Had the Minister of Great Britain employed me to write, can it be supposed that he would not furnish me with the means of living well, without becoming the retailer of my own works? Can it be supposed, that he would have suffered me ever to appear on the scene? It must be a very poor king that he serves, if he could not afford me more than I can get by keeping a book-shop. An ambassador from a king of the gypsies, could not have acted a meaner part. What! where was all the " gold of " Pitt "? That gold which tempted, according to the democrats, an American Envoy to sell his country, and two-thirds of the Senate to ratify the bargain: that gold which, according to the Con-

vention of France, has made one half of that nation
cut the throats of the other half; that potent gold
could not keep Peter Porcupine from standing be-
hind a counter, to sell a pen-knife, or a quire of
paper!

Must it not be evident, too, that the keeping of
a shop would take up a great part of my time?
Time that was hardly worth a paying for at all, if
it was not of higher value than the profits on a few
pamphlets. Every one knows that the Censor has
been delayed, on account of my entering on business; would the Minister of Great Britain have
suffered this, had I been in his pay? No; I repeat,
that it is downright stupidity to suppose, that he
would ever have suffered me to appear at all, had
he even felt in the least interested in the fate of my
works, or the effect they might produce. He must
be sensible, that, seeing the unconquerable prejudices existing in this country, my being known
to be an Englishman, would operate weightily
against whatever I might advance. I saw this very
plainly myself; but, as I had a living to get, and
as I had determined on this line of business, such
a consideration was not to awe me into idleness,
or make me forego any other advantages that I
had reason to hope I should enjoy.

The notion of my being in British pay, arose
from my having now-and-then taken upon me, to
attempt a defence of the character of that nation,
and of the intentions of its government towards
the United States. But, have I ever teazed my
readers with this, except when the subject neces-

sarily demanded it? And if I have given way to my indignation, when a hypocritical political divine attempted to degrade my country, or when its vile calumniators called it " an insular Bastile," what have I done more than every good man in my place would have done? What have I done more than my duty; than obeyed the feelings of my heart? When a man hears his country reviled, does it require that he should be paid for speaking in its defence?

Besides, had my works been intended to introduce British influence, they would have assumed a more conciliating tone. The author would have flattered the people of this country, even in their excesses; he would have endeavoured to gain over the enemies of Britain by smooth and soothing language; he would have " stooped to conquer; " he would not, as I have done, rendered them hatred for hatred, and scorn for scorn.

My writings, the first pamphlet excepted, have had no other object than that of keeping alive an attachment to the constitution of the United States, and the inestimable man who is at the head of the government, and to paint in their true colours those who are the enemies of both; to warn the people, of all ranks and descriptions, of the danger of admitting among them the anarchical and blasphemous principles of the French revolutionists, principles as opposite to those of liberty as hell is to heaven. If, therefore, I have written at the instance of a British agent, that agent must most certainly deserve the thanks of all the real

friends of America. But, say some of the half democrats, what right have you to meddle with the
defence of our government at all?—The same right
that you have to exact my obedience to it, and my
contribution towards its support. Several Englishmen, not so long in the country as I had been,
served in the militia against the western rebels,
and, had I been called on, I must have served too.
Surely a man has a right to defend with his pen,
that which he may be compelled to defend with a
musquet.

As to the real, bloody, cut-throats, they carry
their notion of excluding me from the use of the
press still further. " While," says one of them,
" while I am a friend to the *unlimited* freedom of
" the press, when exercised by *an American*, I am
" an implacable foe to its prostitution to a *foreigner*,
" and would at any time assist in hunting out of
" society, any meddling foreigner who should dare
" to interfere in our politics. I hope the apathy
" of our *brethren* of Philadelphia will no longer be
" indulged, and that an exemplary *vengeance* will
" soon burst upon the head of such a presumptu-
" ous fellow.——*Justice, honour*, national *gratitude*,
" all call for it.——May it no longer be delayed.

"An American."

Are not you, Mr. Swanwick, the President of the
Emigration Society? Well, then, Sir, as your in-
stitution is said to be for the information of persons
emigrating from foreign countries, be so good as
to insert the little extract, above quoted, in your

next dispatches for a cargo of emigrants. Above all, Sir, be sure to tell those who are disposed to emigrate from England, those martyrs in the cause of liberty; be sure to tell them that this is the land of *equal* liberty; that here, and here alone, they will find the true unlimited freedom of the press, but that, if they dare to make use of it, "*justice,* " *honour,* national *gratitude,* will call for exemplary " *vengeance* on their heads."

I should not have noticed this distinction between *foreigners* and *Americans,* had I not perceived, that several persons, who are, generally speaking, friends to their country, seem to think that it was impertinent in me to meddle with the politics here, because I was an Englishman. I would have these good people to recollect, that the laws of this country hold out to foreigners an offer of all that liberty of the press which Americans enjoy, and that, if this liberty be abridged, by whatever means it may be done, the laws and the constitution, and all together, is a mere cheat; a snare to catch the credulous and enthusiastic of every other nation; a downright imposition on the world. If people who emigrate hither have not a right to make use of the liberty of the press, while the natives have, it is very ill done to call this a country of *equal* liberty. *Equal,* above all epithets, is the most improper that can be applied to it; for, if none but Americans have access to the press, they are their masters, and foreigners are their subjects, nay their slaves. An honourable and comfortable situation, upon my word! The emigrants from some countries may be content with it, perhaps: I would not say, that the " Martyrs in the cause of liberty " from England, would not quietly bend beneath the yoke, as, indeed, they are in duty bound to do; but, for my part, who have not the ambition to aspire to the crown of martyrdom, I must and I will be excused. Either the laws shall be altered, or I will continue to avail myself of the liberty that they held out to me, and that partly tempted me to the country. When an act is passed for excluding Englishmen from exercising their talents, and from promulgating what they write, then will I desist; but, I hope, when that time arrives, no act will be passed to prevent people from emigrating back again.

Before I conclude, it seems necessary to say a word or two about the miserable shift which the demccrats have had recourse to, respecting the infamous letter of *Citizen Hint*. They now pretend, that I fabricated it myself, though I have publicly declared, that it was delivered into my hands by a gentleman of reputation, whose name I have mentioned. Can any one be stupid enough to imagine, that I would, particularly at this time, have run the risk of being detected in such a shameful business? And, how could it have been undertaken without running that risk? Had I written it myself, there would have been my hand-writing against me, and had I employed another, that other might have betrayed me; he might have ruined me in the opinion of all those, whom it is my interest as well as my pride to be esteemed by; or, at best, I

should have been at his mercy for ever afterwards.

Besides the great risk of detection, let any one
point out, if he can, what end I could propose to
myself by such a device. As to making my shop
and myself known, I presume I did not stand in
need of a Scare-Crow, to effect that, when the kind
democrats themselves had published to the whole
Union, that I had taken the house in which I live,
for the purpose of retailing my " poison," as they
called it, and had even had the candour to tell the
world, that I had paid my rent in advance.* They
affect to believe, sometimes, that the letter was a
mere trick to bring in the pence, and, in one of
their latest paragraphs, they call me a " catch-
" penny author." But, let them recollect, that

---

* It was to Mr Franklin Bache's creditable and incorrupt-
ible Gazette, that I was indebted for this volunteer advertisement.   This was generous in a declared foe; but those
will not be astonished at the editor's candour and *tolerating
principles*, who are acquainted with the following anecdote.

From the European Magazine, for September 1795, *page* 156.

" When Voltaire arrived at Paris, an interview took place
" between him and Franklin. After the first compliments,
" which by the way were more adulative than comported
" with the character of an American, and above all of a stern
" Republican, the Doctor presented his grandson to Vol-
" taire, in soliciting him for his *blessing*. The philosopher of
" impiety relished the pleasantry; and to render the farce
" complete, he rose from his chair, and with a patriarchal
" air, laid his hands on the head of *the child*, and solemnly
" pronounced, in a loud voice, these three words: *God*,
" *Liberty*, and *Toleration*. All the pious were shocked at the
" American, who, they said, burlesqued Religion in asking
" the *blessing* of Voltaire."

I am now a bookseller, whose trade it is to get money; and if I am driven to such shift as the Scare-Crow, to get a living, let them reconcile this circumstance with their assertions concerning my being liberally paid by Great Britain. A man in British pay, rolling in " the gold of Pitt," could certainly never be so reduced as to venture every thing for the sake of collecting a few eleven-penny bits. It is the misfortune of the democrats ever to furnish arguments against themselves.

Those who reason upon the improbability of the democrats sending the threatening letter, do not recollect the extract I have above quoted from the *Aurora*, in which the people of Philadelphia are called upon to murder me, and are told, that "*jus-* "*tice, honour,* and national *gratitude* demand it." Is it very improbable that men, capable of writing paragraphs like this, should, upon finding the people deaf to their *honourable* insinuations, attempt to intimidate my landlord by a cut-throat letter?

Their great object is to silence me, to this all their endeavours point: lies, threats, spies and informers, every engine of Jacobinical invention is played off. I am sorry to tell them, that it is all in vain, for I am one of those whose obstinacy increases with opposition.

I have now to apologize to my indulgent reader, for having taken up so much of his time with subjects relating chiefly to myself. The task has, to me, been a very disagreeable one; but it was become necessary, as well for the vindication of my own character as for the satisfaction of my friends;

yes, in spite of envy, malice and falsehood, I say, my numerous and respectable friends, who, I trust, will be well pleased to find, that there is nothing in the history of Peter Porcupine to raise a blush for the commendations they have bestowed on his works, or to render them unworthy of their future support.

END OF THE LIFE OF PORCUPINE

THE

SCARE-CROW

BEING

AN INFAMOUS LETTER

SENT TO

MR. JOHN OLDDEN

THREATENING DESTRUCTION TO HIS HOUSE,

AND VIOLENCE TO THE PERSON OF HIS

TENANT, WILLIAM COBBETT.

WITH

REMARKS ON THE SAME

E

THE PREFACE

In the Spring of the year 1796, I took a house in Second Street, Philadelphia, for the purpose of carrying on the bookselling business, which I looked upon as being at once a means of getting money, and of propagating writings against the French. I went into my house in May, but the shop could not be gotten ready for some time; and from one delay and another, I was prevented from opening till the second week in July.

Till I took this house, I had remained almost entirely unknown, as a writer. A few persons did, indeed, know that I was the person, who had assumed the name of PETER PORCUPINE; but the fact was by no means a matter of notoriety. The moment, however, that I had taken a lease of a large house, the transaction became a topic of public conversation, and the eyes of the Democrats and the French, who still lorded it over the city, and who owed me a mutual grudge, were fixed upon me.

I thought my situation somewhat perilous. Such truths as I had published, no man had dared to utter, in the United States, since the rebellion. I knew that these truths had mortally offended the leading men amongst the Democrats, who could, at any time, muster a mob quite sufficient to destroy my house, and to murder me. I had not a friend, to whom I could look with any reasonable hope of receiving efficient support; and, as to the *law*, I had seen too much of republican justice, to expect anything but persecution from that quarter. In short, there were, in Philadelphia, about ten thousand persons, all of whom would have rejoiced to see me murdered; and there might, probably, be two thousand, who would have been very sorry for it; but not above fifty of whom would have stirred an inch to save me.

As the time approached for opening my shop, my friends grew more anxious for my safety. It was recommended to me, to be cautious how I exposed, at my window, any thing that might provoke the people; and, above all, not to put up any *aristocratical portraits*, which would certainly cause my windows to be demolished.

I saw the danger; but also saw, that I must, at once, set all danger at defiance, or live in everlasting subjection to the prejudices and caprice of the democratical mob. I resolved on the former; and, as my shop was to open on a Monday morning, I employed myself all day on Sunday, in preparing an exhibition, that I thought would put the courage and the power of my enemies to the test. I put up in my windows, which were very large, all the portraits that I had in my possession of *kings*, *queens*, *princes*, and *nobles*. I had all the English Ministry; several of the Bishops and Judges; the most famous Admirals; and, in short, every picture that I thought likely to excite rage in the enemies of Great Britain.

Early on the Monday morning, I took down my shutters. Such a sight had not been seen in Philadelphia for twenty years. Never since the beginning of the rebellion, had any one dared to hoist at his window the portrait of George the Third.

In order to make the test as perfect as possible, I had put up some of the " *worthies of the Revolution,*" and had found out fit companions for them. I had coupled *Franklin* and *Marat* together; and, in another place, *M'Kean* and *Ankerstrom.*—The following tract records some amongst the consequences.

THE

SCARE-CROW,

&c.

On the nineteenth instant, Mr. Elmslie, partner of Mr. John Oldden, called on me with the infamous letter, which, without further preface, I shall lay before the reader.

> " *To Mr. John Olden Merchant,*
> " *Chesnut Street.*

" Sir,

" A certain William Cobbett alias
" Peter Porcupine, I am informed is your tenant.
" This daring *scoundrell*, not satisfied with having
" repeatedly traduced the people of this country,
" vilified the most eminent and patriotic characters
" among us and *grosly* abused our allies the French,
" in his detestable productions, has now the aston-
" ishing effrontery to expose those very publica-
" tions at his window for sale, as well as certain
" prints indicative of the prowess of our enemies
" the British and the disgrace of the French. Cal-
" culating largely upon the moderation or rather
" *pucellanimity* of our citizens, this puppy supposes

" he may even *insults* us with impunity. But he
" will e'er long find himself dreadfully mistaken.
" '*Tho* his miserable publications have not been
" hitherto considered worthy of notice, the late
" *manifestation* of his impudence and enmity to this
" country will not be passed over. With a view
" therefore of preventing your feeling the blow de-
" signed for him, I now address you. When the
" time of retribution arrives, it may not be con-
" venient to discriminate between the innocent
" and the guilty. Your property therefore may
" suffer. For depend upon it brick walls will not
" skreen the rascal from punishment when once
" the business is undertaken. As a friend therefore
" I advise you to save your property by either
" compelling Mr. Porcupine to leave your house
" or at all events oblige him to cease exposing his
" abominable productions or any of his courtley
" prints at his window for sale. In this way only
" you may avoid danger to your house and per-
" haps save the rotten *carcase* of your tenant for the
" present."

" A HINT."

" *July* 16th, 1796."

I have copied this loving epistle, word for word,
and letter for letter, preserving the false orthography, as the manner of spelling may probably
lead some of my readers to a discovery of the
writer.

When Mr. Vicesimus Knox (who is a sort of a
Democrat), publishes his next edition of Elegant

Epistles, he will do well to give this a place amongst them; for, it is certainly a master-piece in its way. It will be a good pattern for the use of future ruffians, who wish to awe a man into silence, when they are incapable of resisting him in print. But, the worst of it will be, the compiler will not have it in his power to say, that this was attended with success.

If I am right in my guess, the family of the author of this powder blunderbuss, makes a considerable figure in the Tyburn Chronicle. His grandfather was hanged for house-breaking, and his *papa* came to the southern part of these States on his travels, by the direction of a righteous judge and twelve honest men.

So much for the author; now to his scrawl.

The cut-throat acts in character. He proceeds exactly in the manner of the Revolutionary Tribunal at Paris: that is, he arraigns, condemns and executes, all in the space of about five minutes. The first charge he brings against me is, that I have "repeatedly traduced the people of this coun-"try." I take notice of this, not because it is found in this base and cowardly letter, but because it has long been the theme of all those who wish to decry my performances, and because I am willing to let slip no opportunity of declaring my respect for a public, from whom those performances have ever, from the publication of my first essay, to the present moment, met with the most liberal encouragement.

Let any stupid member of the broken-up, back-

door clubs point out, if he can, one single sentence
in the writings of Peter Porcupine, where the people of the United States are traduced. 'Tis true, I
have not fallen into the beaten track of confound-
ing the good with the bad, of lumping the enemies
and the friends of public happiness together, and
fawning on them indiscriminately. I have not said
that they are all virtuous and wise, and that virtue
and wisdom is to be found amongst them alone.
No; I am no spaniel, nor will I be one. I address
myself to the good sense of my readers, and to that
alone: if they want a buffoon, or whining parasite,
I am not their man.

But, I must do the people of this country the justice to say, that this is not their taste. They stand
in no need of base flattery. Their love of truth
has been fully exemplified in the rapid sale of my
essays, while their contempt for the popular para-
sites has been unequivocally expressed in the fate
of all the miserable attempts that have been made,
to oppose their progress. I have received letters
of thanks, and congratulation from every quarter
of the Union, even from Richmond in Virginia:
and not from " *British Agents*," but from native
Americans, real lovers of their country. I have received offers of service from persons of the first
consequence, in their divers towns and countries,
persons whom I never saw or heard of, previous to
their communications. Let any fawning scribbler
on liberty and equality produce such testimony of
public approbation, if he can.

But, I have, it seems, " vilified some of the most
" eminent and *patriotic* characters amongst us."
'Tis pity, to be sure, that these *patriotic* characters
should be vilified more than they have vilified
themselves. What could I, or any body else, say to
vilify a man, for instance, a man who had made
overtures to sell his country for " a few thousands
" of dollars; " or another, who had done all in his
power, " to stop the wheels of government," by
stirring men up to open rebellion against it? It
is not I who have vilified the *eminent patriots*, it is
Citizen Joseph Fauchet, the old Father Confessor
on the banks of the Schuylkill, when he calls them,
" the pretended patriots of America," and when
he says, they " have already their prices." Surely
I might take upon me to repeat the expressions of
the Minister of France, of our good and faithful
allies, without being chargeable with vilifying the
eminent patriots. And, if I have laughed at little Mr.
Swanwick, what have I done more than every
man, every woman, and every child, in the United
States, at least every one that ever saw his person,
listened to his harangues, or read his poetry? I
wonder what I have done, that I must not laugh,
that I must remain in a corner as demure as
a cat, while every body else are bursting their
sides.

In France, the only country in Europe, (according to *Doctor Jaundice's* account of it), which is *not*
in chains. Under that free and happy sky, the
mild and humane rulers often issue decrees, for-

bidding people to weep or look sad, on pain of death, even at the moment they hear the last groans of their parents; but they have never yet carried their *douce humanité* so far as to forbid men to smile. They permit, nay, encourage, both men and wo-men, to sing and laugh, and cut capers, at the very foot of the guillotine, while the pavement is run-ning with human blood; and yet my cruel and inflexible persecutors will not suffer me to laugh, when I hear them bawling at a civic festival, or see them boxing with an old image that they had formerly adored.

Again, the cut-throat says, I have " *grosly* abused " our allies the French." This is false. By the treaty made between this country and the King of France, the French nation is, in my opinion, no more the ally of the United States, than the Chin-ese are. Louis the Sixteenth was, indeed, the ally, " the *great* and *good* ally " (to make use of the words of Congress) of this country; and, I leave any one who has read my works, to determine whether I have ever abused him or not. The Queen of France, the calumniated Antoinette, was the first foreigner, except some generous Englishmen, that advanced a shilling in the American cause: have I ever abused her memory? It was not I, though it was an Englishman, that cut off her head, and besprinkled her garments with blood, on a sign, hung over a public road. It was not I that guil-lotined her husband, in an automaton, every day, from nine in the morning to nine at night, for the diversion of the inhabitants of Philadelphia.* I did not rejoice at the death of an innocent young prince, whose birth had been celebrated with uncommon pomp in this city, in the prosperous days of his father. I never reviled the gallant French officers and army who served in this country, and to whom America is really indebted; but, on the contrary, I have ever regretted their fate, and expressed my detestation of the barbarians who have dipped their hands in their blood.

The next charge is, I have " the *astonishing ef-* " *frontery* to expose for sale, certain prints, indica- " tive of the prowess of the British, and the dis-

---

* Advertisement, extracted from the Daily Advertiser of the 21st November 1794.

"EXHIBITION,

" *Of Figures in Composition at full Length*,

" (Corner of Second and Callowhill Streets)
" —At the Sign of the Black Bear—

" Late King of France, together with his Queen, taking her last Farewel of him in the Temple, the day preceding his execution. The whole is a striking likeness, in full stature, and dressed as they were at the time.

" The King is represented standing; his Queen on her knees, by his right side, overwhelmed with sorrow, and ready to faint, the King looking tenderly at her.

" Second is the Scaffold on which he was executed, whereon the King stands in full view of the Guillotine; before him is a Priest on his knees, with a Crucifix in one hand, and a Prayer Book in the other; on the side of the Guillotine stands the executioner prepared to do his duty.

" When the first signal is given, the Priest rises on his feet; the King lays himself on the block, where he is secured; the executioner then turns, and prepares to do his duty; and, when the second signal is given, the executioner drops the

" grace of the French." Here the hang-in-chains writer alludes to a print, entitled, " Earl Howe's " Decisive Victory over the French Fleet, on the " first of June, 1794." This print has had a vast concourse of admirers. I had but two of them, one was sold instantly, and I have had more than five hundred applications for the other. What is very singular, is, that one-third part of those who have wished to purchase this print were French Republicans. The print is not sold, nor shall it be. I will keep it in my window, as long as any violence is talked of, and when that ceases, I will have it put in a gilt frame, and hung up in a conspicuous part of my house.

This offensive print is no more than a true representation of the action of the famous *first of*

---

knife, and severs the head from the body in one second; the head falls in a basket, and the lips which are first red, turn blue; the whole is performed to the life, by an invisible machine, without any perceivable assistance.

" *Made by the first Italian Artist, of the name of*

" *C O L U M B A.*

" The workmanship has been admired by the most professed judges, wherever it has been seen.

" ****The proprietors humbly hope for the encouragement of the public, as nothing shall be wanting on their part to render the exhibition *pleasing* and *satisfactory* to their patrons.

" *Price 3s. Children half price.*

" To be seen from 9 o'clock in the morning, until 9 at night."

This exhibition actually continued for several months, and yet no one ever threatened to murder the proprietor.

June, and if it be " indicative of the disgrace of " our allies," it is no fault of mine. If defeat is disgrace, they were certainly most shockingly disgraced on that day. But, I thought it had been long ago agreed on, that, though the fleet got a drubbing, and a pretty decent one too, the victory was, *in fact*, on the side of the French. I am sure Barrere told the French people so; and I am sure most of our Newspapers told the people of America the same story. How many believed them, I will not pretend to say; but if it was a victory, *in fact*, I am treating people with a representation of it, that's all, and am by no means exposing what is " indicative of British prowess."

When William Penn was tracing out his beloved city of Philadelphia; if any one had told him, that the time would come, when a man should be threatened with murder, for offering for sale, in one of the streets, a print " indicative of British " prowess," I much question, if the good man, though a Quaker, would not have said that it was a d—ned lie. Poor old fellow! he little dreamed what was to happen at the close of the " enlight- " ened eighteenth century."

I could turn back to American publications, in which the prowess of Britons is the pleasing theme; in which the French are called, what I never called them, " poor effeminate poltroons." I could bring my readers back to the time, when they set the savages on to scalp the people of these States, and when the people of these States solicited the King of Great Britain to march an army against them.

Has the American Revolution entirely changed the dispositions, affections, and even nature of the two rival nations? Did Great Britain lose every spark of courage, generosity, and virtue, when she lost America? That event certainly could not metamorphose the then inhabitants of the Island, nor could it have any great effect on their children, or at least I presume so. The people of the United States have solemnly declared, in their declaration of Independence, that the British nation are by nature, *just* and *magnanimous*; and will they now swallow their words at the command of the hirelings of the devastators of France?

To return to the print " indicative of British " prowess; " have I not as good a right to exhibit proof of this prowess at my window, as the Democrats have to exhibit the proofs of theirs on the front of the church opposite it? The half-destroyed bust of George II. remains as a monument of their valour, and why should I not be permitted to expose a print to perpetuate the valour of Earl Howe and his gallant fleet? These two pieces are, besides, necessary to the explanation of each other; for when a stranger asks, why the bust of the old king was so unmercifully mangled, the person he addresses himself to, shows him the naval victory of Lord Howe. " There, Sir," says he, " is the fatal " cause." If the impertinent querist goes on, and asks, how George the Second, who died upwards of thirty years ago (and whose bust remained untouched during the whole of the American war) could deserve this rough treatment on account of the drubbing given to the French fleet in 1794, we cut him short at once, by telling him, that he is a rank aristocrat, and totally unfit to live in a land of freedom.

Mr. Oldden is told, that there is but one way left of saving his house, and that is, by obliging me to cease exposing my " *courtly* prints " at my window for sale. It would seem by this, that the cut-throats look upon me as Oldden's vassal; I shall convince them that I am not. To oblige me to desist from any branch of my lawful occupation would prove the toughest job that ever my landlord undertook, should he be silly enough to attempt it. As to obliging me to quit his house, there are no hopes there neither; for I have a lease of it, and a lease that I will hold in spite of all the sansculottes in America.

But what does the cut-throat mean by " *courtly* " prints? " I have Ankerstrom the regicide; that can be no courtly print at any rate. I have, indeed, the portraits of the late king and queen of France; but as they are dead, one would imagine that they could create no alarm. Poor Louis little thought when he sent hither those portraits of himself and his queen, which now hang up in the Congress-House, that the day would come, when a bookseller would be threatened with murder for exhibiting his likeness, in the capital of the Union. Others have exhibited him at their windows, stretched on the scaffold; they had a right so to do; every man to his taste, and I to mine.——'Tis true, I have the portraits of Mr. Pitt and Lord Grenville, and several other noble personages; but then, I have Marat and Lepelletier, by way of rubbing off as I go. I have a Right Reverend Father in God in one corner of my window, and if I could procure the right irreverend Father in the Devil, Tom Paine, I would hoist him up in the other; for want of him I have Doctor Priestley, who, upon a shift, is very capable of supplying his place.

I have some groups, too, executed by order of the French Convention, which, I humbly presume, will not be called " *courtly.*" The taking the Bastile decorates one pane of my window, as it did the Birmingham club-room; the French people on their marrow-bones acknowledging the existence of a God, by order of Robespierre, decorates another; and a third is ornamented with a representation of the glorious " victory " obtained over the Swiss guards, on the 10th of August, 1792. I am promised a print of Poor Richard, in the arms of a brace of angels, who are carrying him off, God knows whither.

I am sure, now, all these things are republican enough; and if my sovereign lords will but please to take my whole collection into view, I cannot think that they will find me so criminal as I have been represented.

And then, there are my books and stationary, almost the whole of which is English. I have been looking round, and cannot for my life find any other American book than Adams's Defence of the American Constitutions, and Peter Porcupine's works. The latter of these my sovereigns have proscribed, and the former speaks about the *well-born*: so that, unless my gracious lords will condescend to permit me to sell these offensive things, I must shut up shop. But, if I must, I hope all the rest of the trade will be compelled to do the same. There is Mr. Campbell has published Hume's History of England, a book as full as it can hold of king's and queen's pictures, and *aristocracy* of all sorts and sizes; and contains, besides, a great number of instances of "British prowess," and of "the disgrace "of our allies." Mr. Dobson too, and Mr. Carey, have published books on *Royal* paper, and Mr. Brown has dared to publish his gazette even on *Imperial*. These are crimes that I have never either committed or attempted. Is not this anti-republicanism to the last degree, and a downright insult on the citizens of the United States?—Again, there is Mr. Young, and several others that I could mention, who have the assurance to expose for sale, Walkden's *Royal British* ink-powder, stamped with the "tyrant George's" arms. Shall all this go unpunished, and shall poor I be eat alive merely for exposing a print or two? Forbid it justice! Democratic justice forbid it!

Nor, should a strict inquisition take place, will the great Mr. Franklin Bache himself come off blameless. He had informed the public, that he is in correspondence with *Peter Pindar*, and it is notorious that this Peter is not only an *aristocrat*, but a declared *royalist*. He has given Tom Paine the severest lashing he ever met with. And as to "tra-"ducing the people of this country," does not

Peter traduce them, when, in speaking of the
United States, he says—

> " Where sons of liberty their pæans sing,
> " And every scoundrel convict is a king."

Is not this traducing the people? And yet Mr.
Bache publicly boasts of his intimacy with this
fellow, and takes infinite pains to propagate his
works! " Birds of a feather will flock together,"
says the old proverb, and it is no more than reasonable to suppose, that Mr. Bache, whatever mask
he may choose to wear, participates in the sentiments of his friend Pindar.

Nay, even Doctor Franklin was an aristocrat,
and an abominable one too, as may be seen in the
very last item of his last will and testament. " I be-
" queath," says he, " to my worthy friend George
" Washington, my gold-headed cane, surmounted
" with a *Liberty-Cap:* if it were a *Sceptre* he is worthy
" of it! " Thus, you see, reader, after all the Doctor's clamour against kings, he thought a Sceptre
something better than a Liberty-Cap. That the
Doctor was sincere here there is no doubt; men
are generally so upon their death-beds, howsoever
profound their hypocrisy may have been through
life.—Poor Richard certainly deserves to be tumbled from his niche for this dying confession, and, I
trust, " when the day of retribution comes," as my
cut-throat terms it, he will not be forgotten. 'Tis
ridiculous, to be sure, to lay violent hands on a
statue; but as this kind of heroism has made a
very considerable figure in this " Age of Reason,"

I do not see why old Lightning-Rod should escape any more than another.

Doctor Priestley, in his first American publication, congratulates himself on being *now* got into a country, where he can publish his sentiments, be they what they may, without any fear of persecution from either *church* or *state*. But he had forgot that there was the democratic gang, more intolerant than either. What will he say, when he sees the letter of my eaves-dropping cut-throat? Will he not begin to repent of having so bitterly complained of the want of liberty of the press in England? One of his excuses for quitting his country was, that he had threatening letters sent to him. Perhaps my cut-throat thinks that all Englishmen are like the Doctor; but he will find himself mistaken: all the stink pots of all the democrats in the western hemisphere shall never drive me from America, nor make me take coach in disguise, as the Birmingham philosopher did.

The democratic societies (for they were then in existence) might, perhaps, have informed Doctor Priestley, that he should be permitted to print whatever he pleased, and, if so, he might well venture to say that the press was free for him; but, unless he had received such previous intimation, his boast of enjoying the liberty of the press was made very much at hazard.

These people plead the liberty of the press, in the fullest extent of the word; they claim a right to print and publish whatever they please; they tell you that free discussion must lead to the truth, and a thousand other arguments they have always ready at their fingers ends to oppose to every kind of restraint. They have calumniated the best of governments and the best of men; they revile all that is good and all that is sacred, and that too in language the most brutal and obscene; and, if they are accused of indecency, or called on for proofs of what they advance, they take shelter in their sanctuary, *the liberty of the press*. But, on the other hand, if any one has courage enough to oppose them, and is so happy as to do it with success; if the mildest of their expressions are retorted, they instantly threaten their opponents with violence and even murder. Their doctrine is, that the press is free for them, and them alone. This is democratic liberty of the press; just such as is enjoyed in that free and happy country whose revolutionary career the people of this country are called upon to imitate.

Much has been said and sung about the Sedition Bills of Mr. Pitt, and the restraint on the liberty of the press in England; but, whatever that restraint may be, it is by law. The law says, that there are such restraints, and, therefore, he who trespasses deserves punishment. The laws of this country say, that the press is free, and we well know what invidious comparisons are continually made between this country and England, in that respect; but, if men are to be murdered, or have their houses burnt for exercising this much talked of liberty, it is time to cease giving it a place among the advantages that the United States enjoy over

the " mother country," as it is sometimes called
in derision. When a foreigner arrives in Great
Britain, he looks at the written law; there he sees
how far he is permitted to carry the use of the
press; and, so long as he keeps within the bounds
prescribed, his person and property is safe. There
is no subaltern power, whose consent he has to
obtain, before he dares publish a book, or expose
a print for sale. His house is not threatened with
destruction, because his window exhibits what is
indicative of the prowess of his nation, and of the
disgrace of their enemies; at any rate, he is not
threatened with murder, for having stepped forward in defence of the laws and the government
of the country.

When I first took up the pen, I found a good deal
of difficulty (as the public will see, one of these
days) to get access to the press at all; not because
the manuscript I offered contained any thing libel-
lous or immoral, but because it was not adapted to
what was supposed to be the taste of the public.
In fact, the press was at the time, generally speaking, as far as related to what is usually termed
politics, in the hands of a daring and corrupt faction, who, by deceiving some, and intimidating
others, had blocked up every avenue to true information. My publications were looked upon as so
many acts of rebellion against this despotic com-
bination, and, therefore, every possible trick was
essayed to discredit them and their author; all
these tricks have, however, proved vain.

My object, and my only object, in writing, was

to contribute my mite towards the support of a government under which I enjoyed peace and plenty. This object I have pursued as steadily as my small share of leisure would allow me; and that I have not laboured in vain, the present conduct of the democratic faction most amply proves. The cut-throat's letter, which I now lay before the public, shows to what a state of desperation they are driven. They at first made some pitiful attempts to answer me; those sunk out of sight, and were forgotten for ever. They then vomited forth calumnies against the author; calumnies so totally void of all truth and even probability, that even their own herd did not believe a word they contained.* Next they published a blasphemous book under my assumed name: this failed also, and the city of New-York has witnessed their shameful defeat as well as Philadelphia. At last, smarting all over with the lashes I had given them, and fearing a continuation, they have had recourse to the poor sneaking trick of a threatening letter. A trick of robbers, who have not courage enough to venture their necks. I have often been congratulated on my triumph over this once towering, but fallen

---

* Among other abominable falsehoods contained in the Aurora concerning me, is my having refused to pay my taxes in this country. To which I answer, that, the small portion of taxes that I have had to pay, has been paid without hesitation. No man, either in a private or public capacity, ever called on me twice for payment of the same sum. The taxes for the property I now rent I have paid up to January next. I owe nobody, neither the State nor the people of the State, a farthing: let the members of the *ci-devant* democratic society say as much if they can.

and despicable faction, and I now possess undeni-
able proof that the triumph is complete.

It is in vain that the cut-throat would persuade
us, that the democrats do not think my " miser-
" able productions worthy of notice; " the very
scrawl of this their stupid secretary proves that
they have dreaded them, and that they yet dread
them. If they despised my " miserable produc-
" tions," why not laugh at them, as I do at theirs?
Why not suffer them to rot on the shelf, like the
Political Progress of Britain, or be kicked about
the street like the Aurora? Threatening Mr. Oldden with the destruction of his house, unless he
could prevail on me to cease publishing, is curious
enough in itself; but it is much more curious,
when accompanied with the observation, that my
publications are *miserable* and *unworthy of notice*.

Of all the stupid inventions that ever entered the
brains of this bungling clan, the cut-throat letter
to Mr. Oldden is the most ridiculous. Had they
studied for years, they could not have found out
any thing that would have pleased me so well. It
will for ever silence their clamours about the liberty
of the press; it will prove to the people most fully,
the truth of what I have always told them; that is,
that these " pretended patriots," these advocates
for liberty and equality, would, if they had become masters, have been a divan of cruel and
savage tyrants. That they know nothing of liberty
but the name, and that they make use of that
name merely to have the power of abolishing the
thing. It will prove to all the world, that they

have long dreaded me, that they still dread me, and that I despise them.

I shall conclude with this unequivocal declaration; that, as to the past, I would not retract a sentence, nor a single expression of what I have written, if the most bloody of the most bloody democrats had his foot upon my breast, and his long knife at my throat; and that, for the future, I will continue to publish and expose for sale whatever I please, and that I will never cease to oppose in some way or other, the enemies of the country in which I live, so long as one of them shall have the impudence to shew his head. Hitherto I have given acids only, I will now drench them with vinegar mixed with gall.

FROM THE FREE PRESS
OF WILLIAM COBBETT,
JULY 22, 1796.

END OF THE SCARE-CROW

REMARKS

OF THE

PAMPHLETS

LATELY PUBLISHED

AGAINST

PETER PORCUPINE

REMARKS

OF THE PAMPHLETS LATELY PUBLISHED AGAINST

PETER PORCUPINE

―――――――

" DEAR FATHER, when you used to set me off
" to work in the morning, dressed in my blue
" smock-frock and woollen spatterdashes, with my
" bag of bread and cheese and bottle of small beer
" swung over my shoulder on the little crook that
" my old god-father Boxall gave me, little did you
" imagine that I should one day become so great a
" man as to have my picture stuck in the windows
" and have four whole books published about me
" in the course of one week."——Thus begins a
letter which I wrote to my father yesterday morning, and which, if it reaches him, will make the
old man drink an extraordinary pot of ale to my
health. Heaven bless him! I think I see him now,
by his old-fashioned fire-side, reading the letter to
his neighbours. " Ay, ay," says he, " *Will* will
stand his ground wherever he goes."——And so I
will, father, in spite of all the hell of democracy.

When I had the honour to serve King George, I
was elated enough at the putting on of my worsted
shoulder-knot, and, afterwards, my silver-laced
coat; what must my feelings be then, upon seeing
half a dozen authors, all *Doctors* or the devil knows

what, writing about me at one time, and ten times
that number of printers, bookbinders, and booksellers, bustling, running and flying about in all
directions, to announce my fame to the impatient
public? What must I feel upon seeing the newspapers filled from top to bottom, and the windows
and corners of the houses placarded, with, a *Blue
Shop for Peter Porcupine*, a *Pill for Peter Porcupine*,
Peter Porcupine detected, a *Roaster for Peter Porcupine*,
a *History of Peter Porcupine*, a *Picture of Peter Porcupine* ? The public will certainly excuse me, if after
all this, I should begin to think myself a person of
some importance.

It is true, my heroic adversaries do all set out
with telling their readers, that I am a contemptible wretch *not worth notice*. They should have said,
not worth the notice *of any honest man*, and, as they
would all naturally have excluded themselves by
such an addition, they would have preserved consistency at least : but, to sit down hammering their
brains for a fortnight or three weeks, and at last
publish each of them a pamphlet about me and
my performances, and then tell the public that *I
am not worth notice*, is such a gross insult to common
sense that nothing but democratic stupidity can
be a sufficient excuse for.

At the very moment that I am writing, these
sorry fellows are hugging themselves in the thought
that they have silenced me, *cut me up*, as they call
it. They think they see me prostrate, and they are
swaggering over me, like a popish priest over a
dead corpse. It would require other pens than

theirs to silence me. I shall keep plodding on in my old way, as I used to do at plough; and I think it will not be looked upon as any very extraordinary trait of vanity to say, that the *Political Censor* will be read, when the very names of their bungling pamphlets will be forgotten.

I must now beg the reader to accompany me in some few remarks that I think it necessary to make on each of their productions, following the order in which they appeared.

" A ROASTER FOR PETER PORCUPINE."

What can I say worse of this blustering performance, than that it bears all the internal evidence of being written by the blunderbuss author who disgusted the city with *Rub from Snub*?

" THE BLUE SHOP; or *Humorous* Observations, " *&c.*"

The inoffensive and unmeaning title of this pamphlet is fully expressive of the matter it is prefixed to, excepting that the word *humorous* was, perhaps, never before so unfortunately applied. Every one who has been taken in with this quarter-dollar's worth, whether a friend or an enemy of Peter Porcupine, curses it for the most senseless and vapid piece of stuff that ever issued from the press. The author, I hear, retorts, and swears the Americans are a set of stupid jack-asses, who know not what true humour is. 'Tis pity he had not perceived this before, he might then have accommodated his *humour* to their understandings. It is now too late to rail against their ignorance or want of taste, for, in spite of his railing and fretting, *James Quicksilver* will, by them, ever be looked upon as a most leaden-headed fellow.

" PORCUPINE, A PRINT."

This is a caricature, in which I am represented as urged on to write by my old master King George (under the form of a crowned lion), who, of course, comes accompanied with the devil. The *Jay*, with the treaty in his beak, is mounted on the lion's back, though, by the by, it has ever been said, by the democrats, that the lion rode the *Jay*. His Satanic Majesty holds me out a bag of money, as an encouragement to destroy the idol, liberty, to which he points. The American Eagle is represented as drooping his wings in consequence of my hostility, and America herself, on the same account, weeps over the bust of Franklin. This is almost the only part of the print of which I find fault; for, if by America the people of America be to be understood, I believe most of those who have read my essays will do me the justice to say, that I have endeavoured to make America laugh instead of weep. —As to myself, I am the hero of the piece, I am brought forward to the front of the stage, where the artist makes me trample upon *Randolph's Defence*, the *Rights of Man*, Old *Common Sense*, *Maddison*, *Gallatin*, *Swanwick*, and *Peter Pindar*. How this blundering fellow came to place *Pindar* among the rest I cannot imagine. It discovers a total ignorance of that author's writings, and of my opinion concerning them. Can the American democrats approve, and can I disapprove, of a writer who says of Tom Paine—

  " Paine, in his thirst for reputation,
  " Has written to deserve damnation? "

Can the democrats approve, and can I disapprove, of a writer who speaks of France and of Frenchmen in the following manner?

" Keel up lies FRANCE ! long may she keep that posture !
" Her knav'ry, folly, on the rocks have tost her;
  " Behold the thousands that surround the wreck !
" Her cables parted, rudder gone,
" Split all her sails, her mainmast down,
  " Chok'd all her pumps, crush'd in her deck;
" Sport for the winds, the billows o'er her roll !
" Now I am glad of it with all my soul.

" To BRITAIN an insidious damn'd Iago—
  " Remember, ENGLISHMEN, old Cato's cry,
  " And keep that patriot model in your eye—
" His constant cry, ' *Delenda est Carthago.*'
" Love I the French?—By heav'ns 'tis no such matter !
" Who loves a Frenchman wars with simple nature.

" The converse chaste of day, and eke of night,
" The kiss-clad moments of supreme delight,
  " To love's pure passion only due;
" The seraph smile that soft-ey'd FRIENDSHIP wears,
" And sorrow's balm of sympathising tears,
  " Those iron-hearted fellows never knew.

" Hear me, Dame Nature, on these men of *cork*—
" Blush at a FRENCHMAN's *heart*, thy handy work;
  " A dunghill that luxuriant feeds
  " The gaudy and the rankest weeds:
" Deception, grub-like, taints its very core,
" Like flies in carrion—Prithee make no more.

G

" Yes, FRENCHMEN, this is my unvarying creed,
" Ye are not rational, indeed ;
" So low have fond conceit and folly sunk ye:
" Only *a larger kind of monkey !* "

And yet this is the writer that the learned and sagacious democrats make me trample upon! I think my namesake Peter speaks here like a good honest Englishman, and though Mr. Bache publishes his works, and boasts of being in correspondence with him, I am very far from either trampling on those works or disliking their author.

Perhaps I ought to take some notice of the quarter whence this *caricature* and the *Blue Shop* issued, as it furnishes an instance, among thousands, of that degradation which the first movers in the French revolution have long been, and still are exhibiting to the world. These poor miserable catch-penny pictures and pamphlets are published by a man of the name of *Moreau*, who was one of those whom Tom Paine and his comrades Price and Priestley called, " the great illuminated and illuminating " National Assembly of France."—Goddess of Liberty! and dost thou permit this thy " great illum-" inated and illuminating " knocker-down of Bastiles to wage a puny *underhand* war with one of King George's red-coats? Dost thou permit one of those aspiring " legislators of the universe ! " who commanded the folding doors of the *Louvre* to fly open at their approach, and who scorned to yield the precedence to Princes and Emperors, to dwindle down into a miserable *marchand d'estampes*? If these be thy tricks, Goddess of *French* Liberty, may the devil take Peter, if ever thy bloody cap and pike entice him to enlist under thy banners.

Mr. Moreau, to his other misfortunes, adds that most calamitous one of thinking he can write. He is cursed with the scribbling itch, without knowing how to scratch himself with a good grace. As this is torment enough in itself, I do not wish to add to it by mentioning particular instances of his want of taste and talents. The greatest punishment I wish my enemies, is, that *Moreau* may be obliged to write all his life-time, and that the rest may be obliged to read his productions.

" THE HISTORY OF A PORCUPINE."

This pamphlet is, I am told, copied, *verbatim*, from a chap-book, containing the lives of several men who were executed in Ireland some years ago, names and dates only are changed, to give the thing an air of plausibility.—It is said to be pub-lished by two Scotch lads, lately arrived in the country, and who now live in some of the allies about Dock-street, no matter which.—One of their acquaintances called on me some days after the publication appeared, and offered to furnish me with the book from which it is taken. This offer I declined accepting of.—I shall only add here, as a caution to my readers, that these are the men who are seen hawking about a work in numbers, which they are pleased to call a *History of France*, and who are proposing to publish a *Monthly Magazine*.

"A PILL FOR PORCUPINE."

It is a rule with book-makers, that a title should, as briefly as possible, express the nature of the work to which it is prefixed. According to this rule, *Pill* is a most excellent title to the performance now before me. A *Pill* is usually a compound of several nauseous, and sometimes poisonous, drugs, and such is the *Pill for Porcupine*.

Various have been the conjectures as to the author of this abusive piece. Be he who he may, he has certainly done me a favour in grouping me along with Messrs. Hamilton, Belknap, Morse, &c. I would cheerfully swallow my part of his pill, and even think it an honour to be poisoned, in such company as this.

Since the *sentimental* dastard, who has thus aimed a stab at the reputation of a woman, published his Pill, I have shown my marriage certificate to *Mr. Abercrombie*, the minister of the church opposite me.——All you who emigrate to the United States of America, to enjoy this unrestrained liberty of the press that they make such a fuss about, take care (if you mean to say a word in favour of your country) to bring your vouchers and certificates with you, or they 'll stigmatize you for thieves; your wives will be called whores, and your children bastards!—Blessed liberty of the press!

"THE IMPOSTOR DETECTED."

This pamphlet ought, on every account, to come last: we have seen the rest rising above each other progressively; this of *Bradford's* crowns the whole, caps the climax of falsehood and villainy.

The former part of it bears the assumed name of *Tickletoby*, the latter, that of *Samuel F. Bradford*. It is evident, however, that both are by the same author; who he is, is not of much consequence: it is clear that he acted under the directions of Bradford, and Bradford must and shall answer for the whole.

What every one recoils at the bare idea of, is Bradford's writing a pamphlet *against the works* of Peter Porcupine. Had he confined his attack to my private character and opinions, he would not have so completely exposed himself; but this, I suppose, his author would not consent to; I do not know any other way of accounting for his conduct.

Every one perceives that the letter which Bradford inserts in *Tickletoby's* part of the pamphlet, is nothing but a poor and vain attempt to preserve consistency. However, to leave no room for dispute on this score, and to convict the shuffling Bradford on his own words, I am willing to allow him to be neuter with respect to *Tickletoby's* part, and will take him up on the contents of the letter which he signs. " That I have made use," says he, " of the British Corporal for a good purpose, I " have little doubt—*Dirty water* will quench fire."

Of his *making use* of me I shall speak by-and-by; at present I shall confine myself to the *dirty water*, which is the name he gives my writings.—Now, how will he reconcile this with his zeal to spread them abroad, and with the aukward flattery he

and his family used to bore my ears with? Had I
believed the half of what they told me, I should
have long ago expired in an extacy of self-conceit.
When the Observations on Priestley's Emigration
were published, Bradford and his wife took great
care to inform me of the praises bestowed on them
by several gentlemen, *Doctor Green* in particular,
and to point out to me the passages that gave the
most pleasure. The *first* Bone to Gnaw gave universal satisfaction, they told me: it was read in all
companies, by the young and by the old; and I remember that the sons told me, on this occasion,
how delighted their uncle, the late worthy Attorney
General, was with it; and that he said he should
have loved me for ever, if I had not been so severe
upon the French. Before the New Year's Gift appeared in public, Bradford told me he had read
some pages of it to two of the *Senators*, who were
mightily pleased with it, and laughed very heartily.
While the father was plying me with his *Senators*,
the sons played upon me from the *lower house*.
Several of the members, *their intimate friends*, wanted to be blessed with a sight of me: one wanted
to treat me to a supper, another wanted to shake
hands with me, and a third wanted to embrace
me. I shall name no names here; but I would advise the members of both houses to be cautious
how they keep company with shop-boys and printers' devils.

I could mention a thousand instances of their
base flattery, but it would look like praising myself
in an indirect way. One more, however, I must

not omit. Bradford, in endeavouring to prevail on me to continue the Congress Gallery, related a conversation that had taken place between him and Mr. Wolcot, the present Secretary of the Treasury (and thereby hangs another tale which I will tell by-and-by), who assured him that some of the officers of government did intend to write an answer to *Randolph's Vindication*, but that my New Year's Gift had done its business so completely, that nothing further was necessary. He added, that they were all exceedingly delighted with my productions.

Again, if he thought my works *dirty water*, how came he to beg and pray for a continuation of them? When I gave his son William a final refusal, he urged, with *tears in his eyes* he urged, the loss his father's credit would sustain by it, and often repeated, that it was not for the sake of the *profit* but the *honour* of publishing my works, that made him so anxious to continue.—My wife was present at this interview, and can, with me, make oath to the truth of what I have here asserted.

Nay, if my works were *dirty water*, why did he threaten to prosecute me for *not continuing them*? Dirty water is not a thing to go to law about. Did ever any body hear of a man's prosecuting another, because he refused to bring him dirty water to throw on the public?

After all this praising, and flattering, and menacing, my poor labours are good for nothing. The writings which had given so much pleasure to Doctor Green, that the Attorney General would have loved me for ever for, that charmed all sexes and all ages, that made grave Senators shake their sides with laughter, and Congress-men want to treat and hug me; that were so highly approved of by the officers of government, that it was an *honour* to publish, and that I was threatened with a prosecution for not continuing; these writings are now become *dirty water*!—Say rather, *sour grapes*.

I must, however, do the Bradfords the justice to say, that they very candidly told me, that every body could perceive a falling off, *after the Congress Gallery*. How singular it was, that I should begin to sink the instant I quitted them! Was this because they did no longer *amend my works* for me, or because they no longer pocketed the cash they produced! The Bradfords are booksellers dyed in grain. Heaven is with them worth nothing, unless they can get something by it.

With respect to the motives that gave rise to my pamphlets, I have already stated them, and as to their literary merit, though I have no great opinion of it, yet, after having heard them ascribed to Mr. Bond, Mr. Thornton (not the *language maker*, but the secretary to the English ambassador), Dr. Andrews, the Rev. Mr. Bisset, Mr. Lewis, Mr. Sedgewick, Dr. Smith, and, in short, to almost every gentleman of distinguished talents among the friends of the Federal Government, it would be mere grimace for me to pretend, that they have no merit at all. It is something singular, that the democrats never pitched upon any low fellow as the author; their suspicions always alighted among gentlemen of family, and gentlemen of learning. It is therefore too late to decry my performances as tasteless and illiterate, now it is discovered that the author was brought up at the plough tail, and was a few years ago a private soldier in the British army.

To return to my friend Bradford. Though I am ready to admit him as a neutral in all that is said by *Tickletoby*, I cannot do this with regard to what is ushered into the world as the performance of *Samuel F. Bradford*. This *hatter-turned-printer*, this sooty-fisted son of ink and urine, whose heart is as black and as foul as the liquid in which he dabbles, must have written, if he did write, at the special instance and request of his father; for, the Lampblack says, " a father's wish is a law with me."

After having premised this, making Bradford responsible for what is contained in his letter and his son's, I shall proceed to remark on such parts of both as I think worth my notice.

And first on the grand discovery of the letter to the *Aurora-Man*.—This is a letter which I wrote to the gazette, under the signature of A Correspondent, against the second part of the Bone to Gnaw. The letter, as now printed by Bradford, may, for ought I know, be a very correct copy. I remember the time and all the circumstances well. Bradford, who is as eager to get money into his hands as he is unwilling to let it out again, repeatedly asked me for a *Puff* to this pamphlet. This very son came to me for it as many as half a dozen times. I at last complied; not that I was unwilling to do it at first (for I had bored the cunning grandchild of the cunning almanack-maker several times before), but I could with difficulty spare time to write it.

Puffs are of several sorts. I believe the one now before us, is what is called a *Puff indirect*, which means, a piece written by an author, or by his desire, against his own performances, thereby to excite opposition, awaken the attention of the public, and so advance the renown or sale of his labours. A *Puff indirect* is, then, what I stand accused of, and as I have no argument at hand to prove the moral fitness of the thing, I must, as pleaders do in all knotty points, appeal to precedents. My authorities are very high, being no other than Addison, Phillips, and Pope.

No one that has read the Spectator (and who has not done that?) can have failed to observe, that he published many letters against his own writings, imitating the style and manner of his adversaries, and containing weak arguments, which he immediately overturns in his answer.—Doctor Johnson tells us that, before the acting of PHILLIPS's *Distressed Mother*, a whole Spectator was devoted to its praise, and on the first night a select audience was called together to applaud it. The Epilogue to this play was written by Addison, who inserted a letter against it in the Spectator, for the sake of giving it a triumphant answer. But, Pope's famous puff is a case exactly in point. " He drew a com-
" parison," says Dr. Johnson, " of Phillips's per-
" formance with his own, in which, with an unex-
" ampled and unequalled artifice of irony, though

" he has himself always the advantage, he gives
" the preference to Phillips. The design of aggran-
" dizing himself he disguised with such dexterity,
" that, though Addison discovered it, Steele was
" deceived, and was afraid of displeasing Pope by
" publishing his paper."——Now, what censure
does Lord Chief-Justice Johnson (who, God knows,
was far from being over lenient) pass on all this?
None at all. He calls neither of these authors " *an*
" *Imposter*: " nor can I think he would have done
so, had their puffs been written *at his request*, and
for *his benefit*.

If a puff can ever be construed as an act of mean-
ness, it must be, when its motive is self-interest.
This cannot be attributed to me, as I could get
nothing by promoting the sale of the work. I had
a note of hand for it in my possession; which the
number of copies sold could not augment the
value of.

What impudence must a man be blessed with,
who can usher to the world a puff, which he
wishes should be looked upon as something hor-
ridly villainous, when he himself requested it to be
written, transcribed it himself, and carried it himself for publication?—But here the Bradfords play
a double game. " It was not I *transcribed* it," says
old Goosy Tom; and " a *father's wish* is a law with
" me," returns the young Gosling. But, you hiss-
ing, web-footed animals, is it not between you?—
The puffing for fame belongs to me; but the tran-
scribing and carrying to the press; all the interested part of the business, all the dirty work, lies

among yourselves, and so I leave you to waddle and dabble about in it.

Having dismissed the *Puff*, we now come to the *breach of confidence* in publishing it. There are many transactions which we do not look upon as criminal, which, nevertheless, we do not wish to have made public. A lady, in love with a handsome young fellow, may make indirect advances, by the aid of a third person. This is certainly no crime; but should the confident preserve one of her letters, and afterwards publish it, I presume such confident would meet with general detestation. This is a parallel case so far; but when to this we add the aggravating circumstance of the confident being the original adviser of the correspondence, we are at a loss for words to express our abhorrence. Yet we must go still further with respect to Bradford. He has not only divulged what was communicated to him under this pledged secrecy, and at his pressing request, to serve him; but he has been guilty of this scandalous breach of confidence towards a man, to whom he owes, perhaps, that he is not now in jail for debt.

It is easy to perceive what drove him to this act of treachery. Revenge for the statement I had published concerning the *one shilling and seven-pence-half-penny* pamphlet. He could not help fearing that people would resent this by avoiding his shop. He was right enough; for, though I am an Englishman, and of course, a sort of lawful prey to the democrats, yet they, even they, cannot help saying that he is an abominable sharper. To be revenged on me for this, he published the letter, and has thus done what all impotent vindictive men do, injured himself without injuring his adversary. I hinted that he had taken me in, and in return he betrays me: to the reputation of a sharper, he adds that of a villain.

After this, will any one say that I am to blame, if I expose this stupid, this mean, this shabby, this treacherous family? Do they deserve any quarter from me?—Every one says—no, Peter, no.

They say I lived in a garret when first they knew me. They found me sole tenant and occupier of a very good house, No. 81, Callowhill. They say I was poor; and that lump of walking tallow streaked with lampblack, that calls itself *Samuel F. Bradford*, has the impudence to say that my wardrobe consisted of my old regimentals, &c.—At the time the Bradfords first knew me I earned about 140 dollars per month, and which I continued to do for about two years and a half. I taught English to the most respectable Frenchmen in the city, who did not shuffle me off with notes as Bradford did. With such an income I leave the reader to guess whether I had any occasion to go shabbily dressed.—It would look childish to retort here, but let the reader go and ask the women in Callowhill street about the rent in old Bradford's yellow breeches.

The Bradfords have seen others attack me upon my sudden *exaltation*, as they call it: upon my having a book-shop, and all this without any visible means of acquiring it: whence they wish to make people believe that I am paid by the British government. It is excessively base in the Bradfords to endeavour to strengthen this opinion, because they know that I came by my money fairly and honestly. They were never out of my debt, from the moment they published the first pamphlet, which was in August 1794, till the latter end of May last.* They used to put off the payment of their notes from time to time, and they always had at their tongues' end; " we know you don't want money." And these rascals have now the impudence to say that I was their needy hireling!——'Tis pity, as Tom Jones's Host says, but there should be a hell for such fellows.

It is hinted, and indeed said, in this vile pamphlet, that I have been encouraged by the American government also.—I promised the reader I would tell him a story about Bradford's patriotism, and I will now be as good as my word.—In order to induce me, to continue the Congress Gallery, he informed me, that Mr. *Wolcot* had promised to procure him the printing of the Reports to Congress: " So," added he, " I will print off enough copies " for the members, and so many besides as will be " sufficient to place at the end of each of your " numbers, and *Congress will pay for printing the* " *whole!* " He told me he had asked Mr. Wolcot for this job, which I looked upon as an indirect way of asking for a bribe, being assured that he

---

* At this time they owed me 18 dollars, which had been due for near six months, and which I was at last obliged to *take out in books.*

built his hopes of succeeding, upon being the publisher of my works.—Now, here's a dog for you,
that goes and asks for a government job, presum-
ing solely upon the merit of being the vender of
what he, nine months afterwards, calls *dirty water*,
and who adds to this an attempt to fix the character of government tool on another man. If I
would have continued the Numbers, it is probable
he might have printed the Reports: but this I
would not do. I wanted no Reports tacked on to
the end of my pamphlets: that would have been
renewing the punishment of coupling the living
to the dead.

Sooty Sam, the Gosling, tells the public that I
used to call him a *sans-culotte* and his father a *rebel*.
If this be true, I am sure I can call them nothing
worse, and therefore I am by no means anxious to
contradict him.—But, pray, wise Mister Bradford
of the " political [and *bawdy*] book-store," is not
this avowal of yours rather calculated to destroy
what you say about my being *an artful and subtle
hypocrite?* I take it, that my calling you *rebels* and
sans-culottes to your faces is no proof of my hypocrisy; nor will the public think it any proof of
your *putting a coat upon my back.* Men are generally
mean when they are dependant; they do not, indeed they do not, call their patrons *sans-culottes* and
rebels; nor do people suffer themselves to be so
called, unless some weighty motive induces them
to put up with it.—This acknowledgment of Bradford's is conclusive: it shows at once on what foot-
ing we stood with relation to each other.

He says that I abused many of the most *respectable characters*, by calling them *Speculators*, *Landjobbers*, &c. who were continually seeking to *entrap and deceive foreigners*.—If I did call those men *Speculators* and *Landjobbers*, who are continually seeking to *entrap foreigners*; if I confined myself to such mild terms, I must have been in an extremely good humour. But, young Mister Lampblack, be candid for once and allow me that your father is a sharper. Oh! don't go to deny that now: what every body says must be true.

"How grossly," says the son, "did you frequent-
" ly abuse the *People of America*, by asserting that,
" for the greater part, they were *Aristocrats* and
" *Royalists* in their hearts, and only wore the mask
" of hypocrisy to answer their own purposes."—If young Urine will but agree to leave out *People of America*, and supply its place with, *family of Goosy Tom*, I will own the sentence for mine; and I will tell the public into the bargain, how I came to make use of it.—I entered Bradford's one day, and found him poring over an old book of *heraldry*. I looked at it, and we made some remarks on the orthography. In a few minutes afterwards he asked me if I knew any thing of *the great Bradford family* in England. I replied, no. He then told me that he had just seen a list of new Peers (*English* Peers, reader!) among which was a *Lord Bradford*; and that he suspected that he was of a branch of their family!—As the old women say, you might have knocked me down with a feather. I did not know which way to look. The blush that warmed my

cheek for him then, renews itself as I write.——He
did not drop it here. He dunned my ears about it
half a dozen times; and even went so far as to request me to make inquiries about it, when I wrote
home.—It was on this most ludicrous occasion,
that I burst out, " Ah, d—n you, I see you are
" all *Aristocrats* and *Royalists* in your hearts yet.
" Your republicanism is nothing but hypocrisy."
And I dare say the reader will think I was half
right.—I wonder what are the armorial signs of
Bradford's family. The crest must be a *Goose*, of
course. Instead of scollops and gueules, he may
take a couple of printer's balls, a keg of lampblack
and a jorden. His two great bears of sons (I except William) may serve as supporters, and his
motto may be, " *One shilling and seven-pence half-*
" *penny for a pamphlet.*" All this will form a pretty
good republican coat of arms.

Let it be remembered here too, that my calling
the Bradfords *Aristocrats* and hypocrites, does not
prove me to be a *hypocrite*, a *needy hireling*, or a
coward. As to this last term which young Lampblack has conferred on me, it is the blustering noise
of a poor timid trembling cock, crowing upon his
own dunghill. I hurl his *coward* back to his teeth,
with the addition of *fool* and *scoundrel*. I think that
is interest enough for one fortnight. The father
has served the silly son, as the monkey served the
cat, when he took her paw to rake the chesnuts
out of the fire with.

They accuse me of being given to *scandal*.—If I
had published, or made use of, one hundredth part

of the anecdotes they supplied me with, I should have set the whole city together by the ears. The governor's share alone would fill a volume.—I'll just mention one or two, which will prove, that I am not the first old acquaintance that Bradford has betrayed.——He told me of a judge, who, when he presented him an old account, refused to pay it, as it was *setting a bad example.*——" Ah, righteous " judge! A Second Daniel!"——He told me, that he went once to breakfast with Mr. Dallas, now Secretary of the State of Pennsylvania, and that Dallas said to him : " By G—d, Tom, we have *no* " *sugar,* and I have not a farthing in the world."— " So," says my Lord Bradford, " I put my hand in " my pocket, and tossed the girl a *quarter of a dollar,* " and she went out and got some."——Another time, he said, Mr. Dallas's hair-dresser was going to sue him for a few shillings, when he, like a generous friend, stepped in and put a stop to further proceedings, by *buying the debt* at a *great discount.* ——I forget whether he says he was repaid, or not.

These anecdotes he wanted me to make use of; but these, as well as all the others he furnished me with, appeared to me to be brought forth by private malice, and therefore I never made use of any of them. Though, I must confess, that, in one instance in particular, this was a very great act of self-denial.

From Secretaries of State, Judges and Governors, let us come to Presidents.—Don't start, reader, my bookseller knew nothing against General Washington, or he would have told it.—No; we are now going to see a trait of Bradford's republicanism of another kind.—*Marten's Law of Nations*, a work that I translated from the French for Bradford, is dedicated, *by him*, to the President of the United States. The dedication was written by me, notwithstanding the Bradfords were obliged to *amend* my writings. When a proof of it was taken off, old Bradford proposed a fulsome addition to it; " give " the old boy *a little more oil*," said he. This greasing I refused to have any hand in, and notwithstanding I did not *know how to write*, and was a *needy hireling*, My Lord and Master, Bradford, did not think proper to make any alteration, though I could have no reasonable objection, as it was signed with his name.

While the old man was attempting to wheedle the President and the officers of the Federal Government, the son, *Samuel*, was wheedling the French Minister : the Bradfords love a double game dearly. He spent whole evenings with him, or at least he told me so. According to his account they were like two brothers. I cannot blame Mr. Adet, who undoubtedly must have a curiosity to know all the secrets of Bradford's press. For my part, as soon as I heard of this intimacy, I looked upon myself as being as well known to the French Minister as I was to Bradford.

But, there is a tale connected with this, which must be told, because it will give the lie to all that young Lampblack has said about correcting and altering my works. His design is to make people believe that I was obliged to submit to his prunings. We shall see how this was in a moment. In the New Year's Gift, speaking of the French Minister, I make use of the following words: " not " that I doubt his veracity, though his not being a " *Christian* might be a trifling objection, with some " weak minded people."—The old Goosy wanted me to change the word *Christian* for *Protestant*, as he was a good friend, and might be useful to his son. He came himself with the proof sheet, to prevail on me to do this: but if the reader looks into the New Year's Gift, he will see that I did not yield.

Bradford never prevailed on me to leave out a single word in his life, except a passage in the *Congress Gallery*. " Remember " (says the son in a triumphant manner) " Remember what was erased " from the *Congress Gallery*."——I do remember it, thou compost of die-stuff, lampblack and urine, I do remember it well; and since you have not told all about it, I will.——The passage erased contained some remarks on the indecent and every way unbecoming expression of Mr. Lewis, on the trial of Randall, when he said, that gentleman would have served *his client* right, if they had *kicked him out of the room*. Bradford told me he had a *very particular reason* for wishing this left out, and as it was not a passage to which I attached much importance, left out it was: but, had I known that his *very particular reason* was, that he had engaged Mr. Lewis as his counsellor in a suit which he had just then commenced against his deceased brother's widow and his own sisters, the passage should not have been left out, for him nor for Mr. Lewis neither. I fear no lawyers.——From this fact we may form a pretty correct idea of the *independence* of Bradford's press, when left to his own conducting.*

I think, the further we go the deeper My Lord Bradford gets in the mire. Let us stop the career, then. Let us dismiss him, his sons, his press and his shop, with a remark or two on one more passage of his son's letter. " You " (meaning me) " can declaim and *scandalize* with the greatest hero " of *Billingsgate*, yet, in sober argument and *chastity* " of manner, you are a mere *nincompoop*."——The reader must have observed, that Boileau, Roscommon and Pope, in their poetical rules, always convey the precept in an example; so we see here, that young Lampblack gives us an example of the very manner he decries.——But, a word more about *chastity*: not quite in the same sense, though not so far from it as to render the transition very abrupt. —*Chastity* from the pen of a Bradford! *Chastity* I say, from No. 8, South-Front Street! *Chastity* from the *bawdy-book shop!*——I have no pretension to an

---

* Bradford pretends to detect me in a lie about my having *a press*. I have two now at work for me, and the printers are always paid the instant their work is done. Can a Bradford say as much?——He tells me something about my being *obliged* to pay my taxes. To be sure I am; but did any tax-gatherer ever dare clap his hand on any of my goods or chattels? No; but the land of Thomas Bradford; back-land which he got out of the old soldiers, who were fighting last war while he was a sort of jailer: this land was sold last year *by the Sheriff*, and that to pay the *taxes too*——You see, My Lord Bradford, that you have refreshed my memory to some purpose.

overstock of modesty or squeamishness. I have
served an apprenticeship in the army; yet have I
often been shocked to see what the Bradfords sell.
Not, perhaps, so much at the obscenity of the
books, as at the conduct of the venders. I do not
know a traffic so completely infamous as this. In
London it is confined to the very scum of the Jews.
It is ten times worse than the trade of a bawd: it is
pimping for the eyes: it *creates* what the punk does
but satisfy when created. These *literary panders* are
the purveyors for the bawdy-house.——However,
as far as relates to the people in question, the sons
are not to blame: " a *father's wish* is a law with
" them."

I shall conclude with observing, that though
Bradford's publication was principally intended to
do away the charge of having duped me in the one
and seven pence half-penny job, he has left it just
as it was. His son, has, indeed, attempted to be-
wilder the reader by a comparison between the
prices of the ensuing pamphlets; but what has this
to do with the matter? His father took the *Observations*, was to publish them, and give me half the
profits. Long after, many months after, every copy
of the work was sold, I asked him for an account of
it, which he brought me in *writing*, and in which
my half of the profits was stated at *one shilling and
seven pence halfpenny*, or, about *twenty-one cents*.——
Now, nothing posterior to this could possibly dim-
inish the barefacedness of the transaction. I did
not actually receive the *twenty-one cents*; I threw
the paper from me with disdain; nor did I ever

receive a farthing for the publication in question from that day to this.

I now take leave of the Bradfords, and of all those who have written against me. People's opinions must now be made up concerning them and me. Those who still believe the lies that have been vomited forth against me are either too stupid or too perverse to merit further attention. I will, therefore, never write another word in reply to any thing that is published about myself. Bark away, hell-hounds, till you are suffocated in your own foam. Your labours are preserved, bound up together in a piece of bear-skin, with the hair on, and nailed up to a post in my shop, where whoever pleases may read them gratis.

END OF THE REMARKS

TALLEYRAND

A SPY

THE following is taken from the Boston Mercury, and is said to be derived from an authentic source. —" The Bishop of Autun, who resided some time " in this country, under the name of Talleyrand " Perigord, has informed the Directory of France, " that they need not regard the United States any " more than the State of Genoa, or Geneva; as " our divisions have weakened us down to nothing " in point of strength and exertion as a nation; " and that there would probably soon be a revolu- " tion here, which would tend to throw us entirely " into the French scale; as the partisans of France " were increasing, and would soon turn out of " the Government all the Washingtonian Party, " all of whom were in the British pay."

" In this information he was joined by almost all " the Americans who were before in France, or " have since gone to that country.

" In the mean time, the French party on this " side of the Atlantic are continually exciting the " French Government to acts of hostility against " the United States; and are so desperately deter-

" mined to destroy the British treaty, as to be will-
" ing, for the accomplishment of that purpose, to
" risk our independence, and even our national
" existence."

That the apostate Talleyrand was a spy in this
country is evident from his being afterwards received with open arms by the very men who had
proscribed him. But I have a word or two to say
about this atheistical bishop. First he set up as a
merchant and dealer, at New York, till he had ac-
quired what knowledge he thought was to be come
at among persons engaged in mercantile affairs;
then he assumed the character of *a gentleman*, at
the same time removing to Philadelphia, where he
got access to persons of the first rank, all those who
were connected with, or in the confidence of, the
Government. Some months after his arrival in
this country, he left a message with a friend of his,
requesting me to meet him at that friend's house.
Several days passed away before the meeting took
place: I had no business to call me that way, and
therefore I did not go. At last this modern Judas
and I got seated by the same fire-side. I expected
that he wanted to expostulate with me on the
severe treatment he had met with at my hands: I
had called him an apostate, a hypocrite, and every
other name of which he was deserving; I therefore leave the reader to imagine my astonishment,
when I heard him begin with complimenting me
on my *wit* and *learning*. He praised several of my
pamphlets, the New Year's Gift in particular, and
still spoke of them as mine. I did not acknowledge

myself as the author, of course; but yet he would insist that I was; or, at any rate, they reflected, he said, *infinite honour* on the author, let him be who he might. Having carried this species of flattery as far as he judged it safe, he asked me, with a vast deal of apparent seriousness, whether I had received my education at *Oxford*, or at *Cambridge*! Hitherto I had kept my countenance pretty well; but this abominable stretch of hypocrisy, and the placid mien and silver accent with which it was pronounced, would have forced a laugh from a Quaker in the midst of meeting. I don't recollect what reply I made him; but this I recollect well, I gave him to understand that I was no trout, and consequently was not to be caught by tickling.

This information led him to something more solid. He began to talk about *business*. I was no *flour-merchant*, but I taught English; and, as luck would have it, this was the very commodity that Bishop Perigord wanted. If I had taught Thornton's or Webster's language, or sold land or ashes, or pepper-pot, it would have been just the same to him. He knew the English language as well as I did; but he wanted to have dealings with me in some way or other.

I knew that, notwithstanding his being *proscribed* at Paris, he was extremely intimate with Adet; and this circumstance led me to suspect his real business in the United States: I therefore did not care to take him as a scholar. I told him, that, being engaged in a translation for the press, I could not possibly quit home. This difficulty the lame fiend hopped over in a moment. He would very gladly come to my house. I cannot say but it would have been a great satisfaction to me to have seen the *ci-devant* Bishop of Autun, the guardian of the holy oil that anointed the heads of the descendants of St. Louis, come trudging through the dirt to receive a lesson from me; but, on the other hand, I did not want a French spy to take a survey either of my desk or my house. My price for teaching was *six* dollars a month; he offered me *twenty*; but I refused; and before I left him, I gave him clearly to understand that I was not to be purchased.

I verily believe that, had I had any *flour* or *precious confessions* for sale, I might have disposed of them to good account; and even my pamphlets, though Bradford calls them *dirty water*, I think I could have sold to Bishop Judas for more than *one shilling and seven-pence halfpenny* apiece.

There is no doubt of there being at this moment hundreds of honest missionaries among us, whose sole business is that of spies. They are flying about the country in every direction; not a corner of it will they leave unexplored. They are now much better acquainted with the sentiments of the people of the Union, and know more exactly those who are to be counted upon in case of a war, than either the Federal Government or State Governments.

FAREWELL

TO AMERICA

I SAILED from New York, on my return to England, on the 1st of June, 1800, having ordered a farewell advertisement to be inserted in the public papers the day before. Soon after I began to publish the *Porcupine* in London, an American wrote to me, complaining of my indiscriminating attacks on his countrymen; to this complaint I published the following answer:

SIR,

I shall preface my answer to your remonstrance with an extract from my *farewell address to your countrymen*, which address it is probable you may not have seen.

" You will, doubtless, be astonished, that after " having had such a smack of the sweets of *liberty*, " I should think of rising thus abruptly from the " feast; but this astonishment will cease, when you " consider, that, under a general term, things dia- " metrically opposite in their natures are frequent- " ly included, and that flavours are not more " various than tastes. Thus, for instance, nourish-

" ment of every species is called *food*, and we all
" like food; but while one is partial to roast beef
" and plum pudding, another is distractedly fond
" of flummery and mash; so is it with respect to
" *liberty*, of which, out of its infinite variety of sorts,
" yours unfortunately happens to be precisely that
" sort which I do not like.

" When people care not two straws for each
" other, ceremony at parting is mere grimace; and
" as I have long felt the most perfect indifference
" with regard to a vast majority of those whom I
" now address, I shall spare myself the trouble of a
" ceremonious farewell. Let me not, however, de-
" part from you with indiscriminating contempt.
" If no man ever had so many and such malignant
" foes, no one ever had more friends, and those
" more kind, more sincere, and more faithful. If
" I have been unjustly vilified by some, others
" have extolled me far beyond my merits; if the
" savages of the city have scared my children in
" the cradle, those children have, for their father's
" sake, been soothed and caressed by the affection-
" ate, the gentle, the generous inhabitants of the
" country, under whose roofs I have spent some of
" the happiest hours of my life.

" *Thus* and *thus*, Americans, will I ever speak of
" you. In a very little time, I shall be beyond the
" reach of your friendship, or your malice; be-
" yond the hearing of your commendations or
" your curses; but being out of your power will
" alter neither my sentiments nor my work. As I
" have never spoken any thing but truth to you, so

" I will never speak any thing but truth of you:
" the heart of a Briton revolts at an emulation in
" baseness; and though you have, as a nation,
" treated me most ungratefully and unjustly, I
" scorn to repay you with ingratitude and injustice.

" To my friends, who are also the real friends of
" America, I wish that peace and happiness which
" virtue ought to ensure, but which, I greatly
" fear, they will not find; and as to my enemies,
" I can wish them no severer scourge than that
" which they are preparing for themselves and
" their country. With this I depart for my native
" land, where neither the moth of *Democracy*, nor
" the rust of *Federalism* doth corrupt, and where
" thieves do not, with impunity, break through
" and steal five thousand dollars at a time."

THE

COURT-MARTIAL

THE object of my quitting the army, to which I was, perhaps, more attached than any man that ever lived in the world; was, to bring certain officers to justice for having, in various ways, *wronged both the public and the soldier.* With this object in view, I went strait to London, the moment I had obtained my liberty and secured my *personal safety,* which, as you will readily conceive, would not have been the case if I had not first got my discharge.——I must here go back a little, and give an account of the measures, which, while in the regiment, I had taken, preparatory to this prosecution; and, in order to give the reader a full view of all the circumstances; in order that he may be able to form a just opinion of what I was in the army, I will give him a short account of my progress.——I enlisted at Chatham in 1784; I joined the regiment, in Nova Scotia, in 1785; I was almost immediately made a Corporal; in a few months afterwards I was made a Serjeant; and, at the end of about a year and a half, I was made the Serjeant Major.——While I was a corporal I was made *clerk* to the regiment. In a very short time, the whole of the business, in that way, fell into my hands; and, at the end of about a year, neither adjutant, pay-master, or quarter-master, could move an inch without my assistance. The *military* part of the regiment's affairs fell under my care in like manner. About this time, the new *discipline*, as it was called; that is to say, the mode of handling the musket, and of marching, &c. called " *Dun-* " *das's System*," was sent out to us, in little books, which were to be studied by the officers of each regiment, and the rules of which were to be immediately conformed to.——Though any old woman might have written such a book; though it was excessively foolish, from beginning to end; still, it was to be complied with; it ordered and commanded a *total change*, and this change was to be completed before the next annual review took place.——To make this change was left to me, who was not then twenty years of age, while not a single officer in the regiment paid the least attention to the matter; so, that when the time came for the annual review, I, then a *corporal*, had to give lectures of instruction to the officers themselves, the colonel not excepted; and, for several of them, if not for all of them, I had to make out, upon large cards, which they bought for the purpose, little plans of the position of the regiment, together with lists of the words of command, which they had to give in the field.——Is it any wonder, that we experience *defeats*? There was I, at the review, upon the flank of the Grenadier Company, with my worsted shoulder-knot, and my great, high, coarse, hairy cap; confounded in the ranks amongst other men, while those who were commanding me to move my hands or my feet, thus or thus, were, in fact, uttering words, which I had taught them; and were, in every thing excepting mere authority, my inferiors; and ought to have been commanded by me.—It was impossible for reflections of this sort not to intrude themselves; and, as I advanced in experience, I felt less and less respect for those, whom I was compelled to obey. One suffers injustice from men, of great endowments of mind, with much less of heart-burning than from men, whom one cannot help despising; and, if my officers had been men of manifest superiority of mind, I should, perhaps, not have so soon conceived the project of bringing them, or some of them, at least, to shame and punishment for the divers flagrant breaches of the law, committed by them, and for their manifold, their endless, wrongs against the soldiers and against the public.——This project was conceived so early as the year 1787, when an affair happened, that first gave me a full insight into regimental justice. It was shortly this: that the Quarter Master, who had the issuing of the men's provisions to them, *kept about a fourth part of it to himself.* This, the old serjeants told me, had been the case *for many years*; and, they were quite astonished and terrified at the idea of my complaining of it. This I did, however; but, the reception I met with convinced me, that I must never make another complaint, 'till I

I

got safe to England, and safe out of the reach of that most curious of courts, a *Court Martial*.—— From this time forward, I began to collect materials for an exposure, upon my return to England. I had ample opportunities for this, being the keeper of all the books, of every sort, in the regiment, and knowing the whole of its affairs better than any other man. But, the winter previous to our return to England, I thought it necessary to make extracts from books, lest the books themselves should be destroyed. And, here begins the history of the famous *Court Martial*. In order to be able to *prove* that these extracts were correct, it was necessary that I should have a *witness* as to their being *true copies*. This was a very ticklish point. One foolish step here, would have sent me down to the ranks with a pair of bloody shoulders. Yet, it was necessary to have the witness. I hesitated many months. At one time, I had given the thing up. I dreamt twenty times, I dare say, of my papers being discovered, and of my being tried and flogged half to death. At last, however, some fresh act of injustice towards us made me set all danger at defiance. I opened my project to a corporal, whose name was *William Bestland*, who wrote in the office under me, who was a very honest fellow, who was very much bound to me, for my goodness to him, and who was, with the sole exception of myself, the only sober man in the *whole regiment*.——To work we went, and during a long winter, while the rest were boozing and snoring, we gutted no small part of the regimental books, rolls, and other documents. Our way was this: to take a copy, sign it with our names, and clap the regimental seal to it, so that we might be able to swear to it, when produced in court.——All these papers were put into a little box, which I myself had made for the purpose. When we came to Portsmouth, there was a talk of searching all the boxes, &c. which gave us great alarm; and induced us to take out all the papers, put them in a bag, and trust them to a custom-house officer, who conveyed them on shore, to his own house, whence I removed them in a few days after.

Thus prepared, I went to London, and, on the 14th of January, 1792, I wrote to the then Secretary at War, SIR GEORGE YONGE, stating my situation, my business with him, and my intentions; enclosing him a letter or petition, from myself to the king, stating the substance of all the complaints I had to make; and which letter I requested Sir George Yonge to lay before the king.——I waited from the 14th to the 24th of January, without receiving any answer at all, and then all I heard was, that he wished to see me at the war-office. At the war-office I was shown into an ante-chamber amongst numerous anxious-looking men, who, every time the door, which led to the great man, was opened, turned their eyes that way with a motion as regular and as uniform as if they had been drilled to it. These people eyed me from head to foot, and I never shall forget their look, when they saw, that I was admitted into Paradise without being detained a single minute in Purgatory.——Sir George Yonge *heard my story*; and that was apparently all he wanted of me. I was to hear from him again in *a day or two*; and, after waiting for *fifteen days*, without hearing from him, or any one else, upon the subject, I wrote to him again, reminding him, that I had, from the first, told him, that I had no *other business in London*; that my stock of *money was necessarily scanty*; and, that to *detain me in London was to ruin me*. Indeed, I had, in the whole world, but about 200 guineas, which was a great deal for a person in my situation to have saved. Every week in London, especially as, by way of episode, I had now *married*, took, at least, a couple of guineas from my stock. I, therefore, began to be very impatient, and, indeed, to be very suspicious, that military justice in England was pretty nearly a-kin to military justice in Nova Scotia and New Brunswick. ——The letter I now wrote was dated on the 10th of February, to which I got an answer on the 15th, though the answer might have been written in a moment.——I was, in this answer, informed, that it was the intention to try the accused upon *only part of the charges*, which I had preferred; and, from a new-modeled list of charges, sent me by the Judge Advocate, on the 23rd of February, it appeared, that, even of those charges that were suffered to remain, *the parts the most material were omitted*. But, this was not all. I had all along insisted, that, unless the Court-Martial were held in *London*, I could not think of appearing at it; because, if held in a garrisoned place like Portsmouth, the thing must be a mere mockery. In spite of this, however, the Judge Advocate's letter of the 23rd of February informed me, that the Court was to be held at Portsmouth, or Hilsea. I remonstrated against this, and demanded that my remonstrance should be laid before the king, which, on the 29th the Judge Advocate promised should be done by himself; but, on the 5th of March, the Judge Advocate informed me, that he had laid my remonstrance before . . . . . *whom*, think you? Not *the king*, but the *accused parties*; who, of course, thought the court ought to assemble at Portsmouth or Hilsea, and, doubtless for the very reasons that led me to object to its being held there.

Plainly seeing what was going forward, I, on the 7th of March, made, *in a letter to Mr. Pitt*, a representation of the whole case, giving him a history of the obstacles I had met with, which letter concluded thus: " I have now, Sir, done all a man " can do in such a case. I have proceeded regu- " larly, and, I may add, respectfully, from first to " last: if I am allowed to serve my country by pro- " secuting men, who have injured it, I shall do it: " if I am thwarted and pressed down by those, " whose office it is to assist and support me, I can- " not do it: in either case, I shall be satisfied with " having done my duty, and shall leave the world " to make a comparison between me and the men " whom I have accused."——This letter (which, by-the-by, the public robbers have not published) had the effect of changing the place of the Court-martial, which was now to be held in London;

but, as to my other great ground of complaint,
the leaving of the *regimental books unsecured*, it had
no effect at all; and, it will be recollected, that,
without those books, there could be, as to most of
the weighty charges, no proof produced, without
bringing forward CORPORAL BESTLAND, and the
danger of doing that will be presently seen.——
But, now, mark well as to these books; as to this
great source of that sort of evidence, which was
not to be brow-beaten, or stifled by the dangers of
the lash. Mark well, these facts, and from them
judge of what I had to expect in the way of justice.
——On the 22*nd of January*, I wrote to Sir George
Yonge for the express purpose of having the books
secured; that is to say, taken out of the hands, and
put out of the reach, of the parties accused. On
the 24*th of January*, he told me, that HE HAD *taken
care to give directions to have these documents secured.*
On the 18*th of February*, in answer to a letter, in
which I (upon information received from the regiment) complained of the documents not having
been secured, he wrote to me, and I have now the
letter before me, signed with his own hand, that
he would write to the Colonel of the regiment
about the books, &c. " Although," says he, " I
" cannot doubt but that the regimental books *have*
" *been* properly secured." This was on the 18*th of
February*, mind; and, now it appears, from the documents, which the public-robbers have put forth,
that the first time any order for securing the books
was given, was on the 15*th of March*, though the
Secretary *told* me he had done it on the 24*th of*

January, and repeated his assertion in writing, on
the 18*th of February*. There is quite enough in this
fact alone to shew the public what sort of a chance
I stood of obtaining justice.

Without these written documents nothing of importance could be proved, unless the non-commissioned officers and men of the regiment should
happen to get the better of their dread of the lash;
and, even then, they could only speak from memory. All, therefore, depended upon those written
documents, as to the principal charges. Therefore,
as the Court-martial was to assemble on the 24th
of March, I went down to Portsmouth on the 20th,
in order to know for certain what was become of
the books; and, I found, as, indeed, I suspected
was the case, that they had *never been secured at all*;
that they had been left in the hands of the accused
from the 14th of January to the very hour of trial;
and that, in short, my request, as to this point, the
positive condition as to this most important matter,
had been totally disregarded.——There remained
then, nothing to rest upon with *safety* but our extracts, confirmed by the evidence of *Bestland*, the
corporal, who had signed them along with me;
and this I had solemnly engaged with him not to
have recourse to, unless he was first out of the
army; that is to say, out of the reach of the vindictive and bloody lash. He was a very little fellow: not more than about five feet high; and had
been set down to be discharged when he went to
England; but, there was a suspicion of his connection with me, and, therefore, they resolved to keep

him. It would have been cruel, and even per-
fidious, to have brought him forward under such
circumstances; and, as there was no chance of
doing any thing without him, I resolved not to
appear at the Court-martial, unless the *discharge* of
Bestland was first granted. Accordingly, on the
20th of March, I wrote, from Fratton, a village
near Portsmouth, to the Judge Advocate, stating
over again all the obstacles that had been thrown
in my way, complaining particularly that the books
and documents had been left in possession of the
accused, contrary to my urgent request and to the
positive assurances of the Secretary at War, and
concluding by demanding the discharge of a man,
whom I should name, as the only condition upon
which I would attend the Court-martial. I requested him to send me an answer by the next day
at night, at my former lodging; and told him, that,
unless such answer was received, he and those to
whom my repeated applications had been made,
might do what they pleased with their Court-
martial; for, that I confidently trusted, that a few
days would place me beyond the scope of their
power.——No answer came, and, as I had learned,
in the meanwhile, that there was a design to prosecute me for *sedition*, that was an additional motive
to be quick in my movements. As I was going
down to Portsmouth, I met several of the serjeants
coming up, together with the music-master; and,
as they had none of them been in America, I won-
dered what they could be going to London for;
but, upon my return, I was told by a *Capt. Lane*,

who had been in the regiment, that they had been brought up to swear, that, at an entertainment given to them by me before my departure from the regiment, I had drunk " *the destruction of the* " *House of Brunswick.*" This was false; but, I knew that that was no reason why it should not be *sworn* by such persons and in such a case. I had talked pretty freely, upon the occasion alluded to; but I had neither said, nor thought any thing against the king, and, as to the *House of Brunswick*, I hardly knew what it meant. My head was filled with the corruptions and the baseness in the army. I knew nothing at all about politics. Nor would any threat of this sort have induced me to get out of the way for a moment; though it certainly would, if I had known my danger; for glorious " Jacobinical " times were just then beginning. Of this, however, I knew nothing at all. I did not know what *the Suspension of the Habeas Corpus Act* meant. When you have a mind to do a thing, every trifle is an additional motive. Lane, who had enlisted me, and who had always shown great kindness towards me, told me they would send me to Botany Bay; and, I now verily believe, that, if I had remained, I should have furnished a pretty good example to those, who wished to correct military abuses. I did not, however, leave England from this motive. I could not obtain a chance of success, without exposing the back of my poor faithful friend Bestland, which, had I not pledged myself not to do, I would not have done. It was useless to appear, unless I could have tolerable fair play; and, besides, it seemed better to leave the whole set to do as they pleased, than to be made a mortified witness of what it was quite evident they had resolved to do.

Botley, 14 *June,* 1809.

A RETROSPECT

At *eleven* years of age my employment was clipping of box-edgings and weeding beds of flowers in the garden of the Bishop of Winchester, at the Castle of Farnham, my native town. I had always been fond of beautiful gardens; and, a gardener, who had just come from the King's gardens at Kew, gave such a description of them as made me instantly resolve to work in these gardens. The next morning, without saying a word to any one, off I set, with no clothes, except those upon my back, and with thirteen half-pence in my pocket. I found that I must go to Richmond, and I, accordingly, went on, from place to place, inquiring my way thither. A long day (it was in June) brought me to Richmond in the afternoon. Two-penny worth of bread and cheese and a penny-worth of small beer, which I had on the road, and one half-penny that I had lost somehow or other, left three pence in my pocket. With this for my whole fortune, I was trudging through Richmond, in my blue smock-frock and my red garters tied under my knees, when, staring about me, my eye fell upon a little book, in a bookseller's window, on the outside of which was written: " TALE OF A

" TUB; PRICE 3d." The title was so odd, that my curiosity was excited. J had the 3d. but, then, I could have *no supper*. In I went, and got the little book, which I was so impatient to read, that I got over into a field, at the upper corner of Kew gardens, where there stood a *hay-stack*. On the shady side of this, I sat down to read. The book was so different from any thing that I had ever read before: it was something so *new* to my mind, that, though I could not at all understand some of it, it delighted me beyond description; and it produced what I have always considered a sort of birth of intellect. I read on till it was dark, without any thought about supper or bed. When I could see no longer, I put my little book in my pocket, and tumbled down by the side of the stack, where I slept till the birds in Kew Gardens awaked me in the morning; when off I started to Kew, reading my little book. The singularity of my dress, the simplicity of my manner, my confident and lively air, and, doubtless, his own compassion besides, induced the gardener, who was a Scotsman, I remember, to give me victuals, find me lodging, and set me to work. And, it was during the period that I was at Kew, that the present king and two of his brothers laughed at the oddness of my dress, while I was sweeping the grass plot round the foot of the Pagoda. The gardener, seeing me fond of books, lent me some gardening books to read; but, these I could not relish after my *Tale of a Tub*, which I carried about with me wherever I went, and when I, at about twenty years old, lost it in a box that fell overboard, in the Bay of Funday in North America, the loss gave me greater pain than I have ever felt at losing thousands of pounds.

This circumstance, trifling as it was, and childish as it may seem to relate it, has always endeared the recollection of *Kew* to me. About five weeks ago, I had occasion to go from Chelsea to Twickenham with my two eldest sons. I brought them back through Kew, in order *to show them the place where the hay-stack stood*; having frequently related to them what I have now related to you.

Far be it from me to suppose, that *you* want any thing to convince you, that the numerous *foul accusations*, made against me by the public press, are *wholly false*. But, upon this occasion, permit me to say, that it is not unnecessary, and that it is but bare justice to *you*, justice to your discernment and your virtue, for me to show, that you have not conferred such marks of respect on one who is unworthy of them.

You have heard how, and at what an age, I started in the world. Those of you, who are *mothers* will want nothing but the involuntary impulse of your own hearts to carry your minds back to the alarm, the fears and anxieties of my most tender mother. But, if I am " an *extraordinary* man," as I have been called by some persons, who ought to have found out a different epithet, I was a still more extraordinary *boy*. For, though I never returned home for any length of time, and never put my parents to a farthing in expence, after the time abovementioned, I was always a most dutiful son, never having, in my whole life, wilfully and deliberately disobeyed either my father or my mother. I carried in my mind their precepts against *drinking* and *gaming*; and I have never been drunk and have never played at any game in my life. When in the army I was often tempted to take up the cards. But, the words of my father came into my mind, and rescued me from the peril. Exposed, as you must well know, to all sorts of temptations; young, strong, adventurous, uncommonly gay and greatly given to talk; still, I never, in my whole life, was brought before a magistrate, either as defendant or complainant. And, even up to *this hour*, about *five oaths* are all that I have ever taken, notwithstanding the multitude and endless variety of affairs, in which I have been engaged. I entered the army at *sixteen*, and quitted it at *twenty five*. I never was once even *accused* of a fault of any sort. At *nineteen* I was promoted to *Serjeant-Major* from a Corporal, over the heads of nearly fifty serjeants. While my regiment was abroad, I received the public and official thanks of the Governor of the Province for my zeal in the King's service; while no officer in the regiment received any thanks at all. Many years after this, this same Governor (General Carleton) came to see me and to claim the pleasure of my acquaintance. When I quitted the army at Portsmouth, I had a discharge, bearing on it, that I had been discharged at my own request, *and in consequence of the great services I had rendered the king's service in that regiment*. During this part of my life I lived amongst, and was compelled to associate with, the most beastly of drunkards, where liquor was so cheap, that even a soldier might be drunk every day; yet I never, during the whole time, even *tasted* of any of that liquor. My father's, and more especially my mother's precepts were always at hand to protect me.

In 1792, I went to the United States of America. There I became a *writer*. I understood little at that time; but the utmost of my ability was exerted on the side of *my country*, though I had been greatly disgusted at the trick that had been played me in England, with regard to a court-martial, which I had demanded upon some officers. I forgot every thing when the honour of England was concerned. The king's minister in America made me offers of *reward*. I refused to accept of any, in any shape whatever. Reward was offered me, when I came home. I always refused to take one single penny from the government. If I had been to be *bought*, judge you, my countrymen, how *rich*, and even how *high*, I might have been at this day! But, I value the present received from the females of Lancashire a million times higher than all the money and all the titles which ministers and kings have to bestow.

London, Feb. 5, 1820.

APPENDIX

I HAVE thought it well to supply, as an appendix to this volume, certain parts of Cobbett's story which are not given in the pieces here reprinted. About his life in the Army much more is written both in articles in the *Political Register* and in his *Advice to Young Men*; and certain passages seem to me worth quoting here as a sort of supplement to the *Life and Adventures*. I could have quoted many more; but these few must serve to guide the reader to the *Advice* itself, if perchance he does not know it already.

Writing of the need for " husbanding well " one's time, Cobbett describes, in the *Advice*, his own habits as a soldier.

" To this, more than to any other thing, I owed my very extraordinary promotion in the army. I was *always ready*: if I had to mount guard at *ten*, I was ready at *nine*: never did any man, or any thing, wait one moment for me. Being, at an age *under twenty years* [really twenty-three], raised from Corporal to Serjeant Major *at once*, over the heads of thirty serjeants, I naturally should have been an object of envy and hatred; but this habit of early rising and of rigid adherence to the precepts which I have given you, really subdued these passions; because every one felt, that what I did he had never done, and never could do. Before my promotion, a clerk was wanted to make out the morning report of the regiment. I rendered the clerk unnecessary; and, long before any other man was dressed for the parade, my work for the morning was all done, and I myself was on the parade, walking, in fine weather, for an hour perhaps. My custom was this: to get up, in summer, at day-light, and in winter at four o'clock; shave, dress, even to the putting of my sword-belt over my shoulder, and having my sword lying on the table before me, ready to hang by my side. Then I ate a bit of cheese, or pork, and bread. Then I prepared my report, which was filled up as fast as the companies brought me in the materials. After this I had an hour or two to read, before the time came for my duty out of doors, unless when the regiment, or part of it, went out to exercise in the morning. When this was the case, and

K

the matter was left to me, I always had it on the ground in such time as that the bayonets glistened in the *rising sun*, a sight which gave me delight, of which I often think, but which I should in vain endeavour to describe. If the *officers* were to go out, eight or ten o'clock was the hour, sweating the men in the heat of the day, breaking in upon the time for cooking their dinner, putting all things out of order and all men out of humour. When I was commander, the men had a long day of leisure before them: they could ramble into the town or into the woods; go to get raspberries, to catch birds, to catch fish, or to pursue any other recreation, and such of them as chose, and were qualified, to work at their trades. So that here, arising solely from the early habits of one very young man, were pleasant and happy days given to hundreds." [*Advice to Young Men*, section 39.]

Then again, commending the study of grammar to young men, Cobbett writes of his own experience at the regimental depot at Chatham.

" I learned grammar when I was a private soldier on the pay of sixpence a day. The edge of my berth, or that of the guard-bed, was my seat to study in; my knapsack was my book-case; a bit of board, lying on my lap, was my writing-table; and the task did not demand any thing like a year of my life. I had no money to purchase candle or oil; in winter-time it was rarely that I could get any evening-light but that of *the fire*, and only my *turn* even of that. . . . To buy a pen or a sheet of paper I was compelled to forego some portion of food, though in a state of half-starvation; I had no moment of time that I could call my own; and I had to read and to write amidst the talking, laughing, singing, whistling and brawling of at least half a score of the most thoughtless of men, and that too in the hours of their freedom from all control. Think not lightly of the *farthing* that I had to give, now and then, for ink, pen, or paper! That farthing was, alas! a *great sum* to me! I was as tall as I am now; I had great health and great exercise. The whole of the money, not expended for us at market, was *two-pence a week* for each man. I remember, and well I may! that upon one occasion I, after all absolutely necessary expenses, had, on a Friday, made shift to have a halfpenny in reserve, which I had destined for the purchase of a *red-herring* in the morning; but, when I pulled off my clothes at night, so hungry then as to be hardly able to endure life, I found that I had *lost my halfpenny*! I buried my head under the miserable sheet and rug, and cried like a child!" [*Advice to Young Men*, section 44.]

The reader will probably conclude, and conclude correctly, that Cobbett must have been as strong in mind as in body, and in body as in mind. He could place immense tasks on himself without feeling the strain; his vitality was inexhaustible.

It would, however, be quite wrong to conclude that Cobbett did nothing but work. He "used, both in France and America, to *romp* most famously with the girls" that came in his way. In New Brunswick, he often went hunting, and "took great delight" in rambles through the woods. He was always companionable, and made close friends wherever he went. He took his full share in the "jaunting and dancing" that went on among the New Brunswick settlers. And, during his stay there, he found time also for a characteristic courtship of Ann Reid, who afterwards became his wife.

"When I first saw my wife, she was *thirteen years old*, and I was within about a month of *twenty-one* [really twenty-four]. She was the daughter of a Serjeant of artillery, and I was the Serjeant-Major of a regiment of foot, both stationed at forts near the city of St. John, in the Province of New Brunswick. I sat in the same room with her, for about an hour, in company with others, and I made up my mind that she was the very girl for me. That I thought her beautiful was certain, for that I had always said should be an indispensable qualification; but I saw in her what I deemed marks of that sobriety of *conduct* of which I have said so much, and which has been by far the greatest blessing of my life. It was now dead winter, and, of course, the snow several feet deep on the ground, and the weather piercing cold. It was my habit, when I had done my morning's writing, to go out at break of day to take a walk on a hill at the foot of which our barracks lay. In about three mornings after I had first seen her, I had, by an invitation to breakfast with me, got up two young men to join me in my walk; and our road lay by the house of her father and mother. It was hardly light, but she was out on the snow, scrubbing out a washing-tub. 'That's the girl for me,' said I, when we had got out of her hearing. One of these young men came to

England soon afterwards; and he, who keeps an inn in Yorkshire, came over to Preston, at the time of the election, to verify whether I were the same man. When he found that I was, he appeared surprised; but what was his surprise, when I told him that those tall young men, whom he saw around me, were the *sons* of that pretty little girl that he and I saw scrubbing out the washing-tub on the snow in New Brunswick at day-break in the morning!" [*Advice to Young Men*, section 94.]

Cobbett had made up his mind. "From the day that I first spoke to her, I never had a thought of her ever being the wife of any other man, more than I had a thought of her being transformed into a chest of drawers." A few months later, his regiment was moved to Frederickton, a hundred miles away up the river, and, a little later, the artillery were ordered back to England, and Ann Reid went with them. Cobbett sent her all his savings, a hundred and fifty guineas, to take care of, telling her to use them if she needed money before he could get back to England and marry her. Meanwhile, his regiment was kept in New Brunswick two years beyond its time, and his love for Ann Reid had a severe testing.

On one of his rambles up country, he got lost and found refuge in the house of one of the " Yankee Loyalists " of New Brunswick.

> "The master and mistress of the house, aged about fifty, were like what an English farmer and his wife were half a century ago. There were two sons, tall and stout, who appeared to have come in from work, and the youngest of whom was about my age, then twenty-three [twenty-six]. But there was *another member* of the family, aged nineteen, who (dressed according to the neat and simple fashion of New England, whence she had come with her parents six or seven years before) had her long light-brown hair twisted nicely up, and fastened on the top of her head, in which head were a pair of lively blue eyes, associated with features of which that softness and that sweetness, so characteristic of American girls, were the predominant expressions, the whole being set off by a complexion indicative of glowing health, and forming, figure, movements, and all taken together, an assemblage of beauties, far surpassing any that I had ever seen but *once* in my life. That *once* was, too, *two years agone*; and, in such a case and at such an age, two years, two whole

years, is a long, long while." [*Advice to Young Men,* section 146.]

Cobbett tore himself away, hardly and not without some sense of shame, from the close intimacy which grew out of this encounter. When at last his regiment was ordered home, he bade his friends farewell with an aching and even a remorseful heart. Arrived in England, he immediately sought out Ann Reid. " I found my little girl *a servant of all work* (and hard work it was), at *five pounds a year*, in the house of a Captain Brisac; and, without hardly saying a word about the matter, she put into my hands *the whole of my hundred and fifty guineas unbroken !* "

William Cobbett and Ann Reid were married at Woolwich on the fifth of February, 1792. His wife accompanied him to France, and followed him to the United States as soon as he was safely settled there.

" I began my young marriage days in and near Philadelphia. At one of those times to which I have just alluded, in the middle of the burning hot month of July, I was greatly afraid of fatal consequences to my wife for want of sleep, she not having, after the great danger was over, had any sleep for more than forty-eight hours. All great cities, in hot countries, are, I believe, full of dogs; and they, in the very hot weather, keep up, during the night, a horrible barking and fighting and howling. Upon the particular occasion to which I am adverting, they made a noise so terrible and so unremitted, that it was next to impossible that even a person in full health and free from pain should obtain a minute's sleep. I was, about nine in the evening, sitting by the bed: ' I do think,' said she, ' that I could go to sleep *now*, if it were not *for the dogs*.' Down stairs I went, and out I sallied, in my shirt and trowsers, and without shoes and stockings; and, going to a heap of stones lying beside the road, set to work upon the dogs, going backward and forward, and keeping them at two or three hundred yards' distance from the house. I walked thus the whole night, barefooted, lest the noise of my shoes might possibly reach her ears; and I remember that the bricks of the causeway were, even in the night, so hot as to be disagreeable to my feet. My exertions produced the desired effect: a sleep of several hours was the consequence; and, at eight o'clock in the morning, off went I to a day's business, which was to end at six in the evening." [*Advice to Young Men*, section 166.]

A final extract must serve to present the picture of Cobbett's private life during these early years of his marriage.

" Till I had a second child, no servant ever entered my house, though well able to keep one; and never, in my whole life, did I live in a house so clean, in such trim order, and never have I eaten or drunk, or slept or dressed, in a manner so perfectly to my fancy, as I did then. I had a great deal of business to attend to, that took me a great part of the day from home; but, whenever I could spare a minute from business, the child was in my arms; I rendered the mother's labour as light as I could; any bit of food satisfied me; when watching was necessary, we shared it between us; and that famous GRAMMAR for teaching French people English, which has been for thirty years, and still is, the great work of this kind, throughout all America, and in every nation in Europe, was written by me, in hours not employed in business, and, in great part, during my share of the night watchings over a sick, and then only child, who, after lingering many months, died in my arms." [*Advice to Young Men*, section 161.]

This domestic interior is really the essential complement to the picture of Cobbett's public activities. To the fierce controversies of his years in America his married life forms a quiet background. While he waged war against Jacobins and Democrats, accused Bradford of commercial swindling, M'Kean of judicial corruption, Rush of medical quackery, he mingled these alarums and excursions abroad with a simple and satisfying felicity at home. His first child died, indeed; but before he left America he had two more, a daughter, Anne, and then a son, William.

Here, then, we may leave William Cobbett. The foregoing pieces present him in an unfamiliar aspect, as the uncompromising enemy of France and Reform, and the upholder of " The Thing " which he was later vehemently to denounce. But, *plus cela change, plus c'est le même homme*; and, now that the old causes set us aflame no longer, we can take him simply as a man, and treat his opinions, though not his attitude, as a matter of environment and circumstance. We can recognise in " Peter Porcupine, of Philadelphia," that William Cobbett, of Farnham, Surrey, who has been long our friend.

NOTES

NOTES TO "THE LIFE AND ADVENTURES OF PETER PORCUPINE"

P. 9. This piece was first published by Cobbett himself at 25 North Second Street, Philadelphia, in August, 1796. It was at once re-issued in England. Some of the later English editions are garbled. The original text is printed in *Porcupine's Works*, vol. iv.

P. 12. *Mr. Bache.* Presumably Richard Bache (1737-1811), proprietor of the *Aurora* newspaper, and father of Benjamin Franklin Bache (1769-1798), its editor and Cobbett's special enemy. Richard Bache was chairman of the Republican Society of Philadelphia, and a leading Democrat. He married Benjamin Franklin's daughter, Sarah. The *Aurora* was one of the chief Democratic newspapers in Philadelphia. Cobbett repeatedly accused the Baches of being in the pay of France, while they countercharged him with being an English agent.

P. 13. "*A certain foreign agent.*" See page 53, and note thereto.

P. 14. *Mr. Thomas Bradford.* The Bradfords were the leading booksellers and publishers in Philadelphia, and active in its public life. The first of the family, William Bradford, was brought over by Penn in 1682 at the founding of Pennsylvania. His grandson, William, founded the *Pennsylvania Journal*. Thomas Bradford (1745-1838) was the son of this William. His brother, William, was Judge of the Supreme Court of Pennsylvania, and in 1794 became Attorney-General of the United States. Thomas Bradford, junior (1781-1851), joined his father in the publishing business. The Samuel F. Bradford attacked in the *Remarks* (see p. 101) is another son of Thomas. The Bradfords were a highly influential family, and Cobbett's attacks on them got him into trouble.

P. 15. *Dr. Priestley.* This is, of course, the famous Joseph Priestley (1733-1804), reformer, chemist and divine. His house was burnt down by the Birmingham mob in 1791.

In 1794 he emigrated to the United States, chiefly on account of his hostility to the repressive policy then in full force in Great Britain. He settled in Northumberland, Pennsylvania, and was much fêted by the Democratic and Radical Societies in the United States. We shall see how their welcome to him provoked Cobbett to take up pamphleteering. See page 43.

P. 16. *Thomas Mauduit*. Thomas Antoine Mauduit du Plessis (1752-1791) was a French adventurer and royalist. Born in Brittany, he travelled widely in the East, and then, in 1780, went to America. He fought at the battle of Brandywine and became a major. As commander of the troops at Port au Prince he opposed the French Revolution and organised royalist volunteers (*Pompons Blancs*), with whose aid he tried to hold the colony. His repressive control provoked an insurrection, and his troops mutinied. Mauduit was killed and mutilated by his own men.

P. 18. *Doctor Franklin. i.e.* Benjamin Franklin, whom Cobbett delighted to attack.

P. 20. *Date of Cobbett's Birth*. Cobbett was really born in March, 1763. He always gives the date as 1766, and therefore mis-states his age in connection with a number of his adventures. His sons, in their edition of his *Political Writings*, gave the date as 1762; but Mr. E. I. Carlyle's researches establish 1763 as correct. See the Appendix to his *William Cobbett*.

P. 26. *Captain Berkley*. George Cranfield Berkeley (1753-1818), afterwards Admiral and Baron Berkeley—M.P. for Gloucester, 1781-1812.

P. 33. *Colonel Debeig*. Hugh Debbieg, afterwards General. He was censured and temporarily deprived of his rank owing to his dispute with the Duke of Richmond, who was Master General of Ordnance in 1789.

Lowth's Grammar. This was long a standard work. Robert Lowth (1710-1787), Bishop of Oxford and then of London, published it first in 1762.

P. 34. *Mr. Swanwick*. John Swanwick, a Democratic politician and a minor poet, was one of Cobbett's favourite butts. He was elected to Congress for Pennsylvania, and there strongly defended the French. He was also an advocate of Women's Rights. For Cobbett's views on his poetry, see *Porcupine's Works*, vol. iii. p. 401, and, for an Open Letter to him, vol. vi. p. 78. " Thus it is to be a pretender to universal genius, without having any genius at all. Instead of getting renown, a man gets himself laughed at."

P. 36. *Lord Edward Fitzgerald*. This is, of course, the Lord Edward Fitzgerald (1763-1798) who was cashiered in 1792 for attending a revolutionary banquet in Paris, and mortally wounded in course of arrest after he had thrown in his lot with the United Irishmen.

P. 38. *Citizen Plato*. " This little gentleman, whom the French ladies call the *garçon fendu*, is said to delight in mischief like a jack-daw. He has amassed a great deal of money together, God knows how, which he appears determined to employ in doing this country all the harm in his power. He fully justifies the maxim of the naturalists, who tell us, that the most impotent reptiles are ever the most malicious. We have, however, this consolation; there will be none of his breed to torment our children." (*New Year's Gift to the Democrats. Porcupine's Works*, vol. ii. p. 468.) " Patriot Plato " 's election to Congress had aroused Cobbett's ire. " Let him speechify in the boarding schools till he is hoarse, but not in a legislative assembly " —this on the ground that he was a " Pope Joan," or eunuch. (*ibid.*)

P. 40. *Raynal*. The Abbé Raynal published his *Tableau et Révolutions des Colonies Angloises dans l'Amérique Septentrionale* in 1781.

P. 41. *Mr. Short*. William Short (1759-1849) went to Paris with Jefferson in 1785 as Secretary of Legation and was Chargé d'Affaires from 1789 to 1792, when he went to the Hague as Minister Resident. He was subsequently Minister at Madrid.

P. 42. *Mr. Oldden*. See for this letter and for Mr. Oldden Cobbett's *Scare-crow*, printed at page 70 of this volume.

P. 43. *Mr. Carey*. Matthew Carey (1760-1839) was an Irishman. He established in Ireland the *Volunteer's Journal*, and was imprisoned by the House of Commons for libel in 1784. On his release he emigrated to the United States, and set up as a publisher in Philadelphia. There he founded the *Pennsylvania Herald*, and in 1793 the Hibernian Society. See *Porcupine's Works*, vol. ix. p. 60, for an attack on him and his brother as " disaffected Irishmen " and supporters of the United Irishmen. Matthew Carey wrote a number of economic tracts in favour of Protection. He was the father of the well-known American economist, H. C. Carey.

P. 45. *The Whiskey-Boys*. The reference is to the " Whiskey

Insurrection " in Western Pennsylvania in 1794. This was a rising against the enforcement of the Excise Law of 1791, under which the illicit stills of the farmers were being suppressed. The rising was easily put down, but created great political excitement. See Cobbett's account of the insurrection in *Porcupine's Works*, vol. i. He sought to represent the rising as " the work of France and her adherents."

P. 46. *Bone to Gnaw for the Democrats*. Cobbett's second important tract, first published in two Parts in 1795. It is reprinted in vol. ii. of *Porcupine's Works*.

P. 48. *Kick for a Bite*. Philadelphia, 1795. Reprinted in *Porcupine's Works*, vol. ii.

P. 49. *Plain English. A Little Plain English, Addressed to the People of the United States*. Philadelphia, 1795. Reprinted in *Porcupine's Works*, vol. ii.

New Year's Gift. A New Year's Gift for the Democrats. Philadelphia, 1796. Reprinted in *Porcupine's Works*, vol. ii.

Prospect. A Prospect from the Congress Gallery. Philadelphia, 1796. Reprinted in *The Political Censor*, Number 1, in *Porcupine's Works*, vol. iii.

P. 50. *Mr. Moreau de St. Mery*. Médéric Louis Elie Moreau de Saint Mery (1750-1819) was born in Martinique, and represented first Santo Domingo and later Martinique in the French National and Constituent Assemblies. Imprisoned in France, with Rochefoucauld, he escaped to America and opened a bookshop in Philadelphia. He wrote works on the Constitution of the French Colonies in America and on Santo Domingo. His *Description of Saint Domingo*, translated by Cobbett, was published in 1796. In 1800 he returned to France and became Councillor of State, but was deposed by Napoleon in 1806. For Cobbett's views on him, see p. 98.

The *Censor. The Political Censor*, Cobbett's first venture into periodical journalism, was published by him in 1796-7. Eight monthly numbers appeared. They were really political pamphlets issued under a collective title.

P. 53. *Mr. Bond*. Phineas Bond (? -1816) was a well-known physician of Philadelphia, and one of the founders of the University of Pennsylvania. In the American War, he took the British side. In 1786 he was appointed British Consul for the Middle States and British Commissary for Commercial Affairs. The Democrats, headed by Madison, opposed his recognition, but he was recognised as Consul only.

P. 53. *Mr. Allen.* Andrew Allen (1740-1825) was born in
Philadelphia and became Attorney-General of Pennsylvania in 1766. He supported the American Revolution
in its earlier stages, but subsequently deserted to the
British side, and later fled to England. His American
estates were confiscated; and he received a pension from
the British Government. His daughter, Margaret, married George Hammond.

    Mr. Hammond. George Hammond (1763-1853) was
sent by Lord Grenville to Philadelphia as Minister-Pleni-
potentiary in 1791, and was thus the first British Minister
to the United States. He was well acquainted with Cobbett later. They met at dinner at William Windham's
after Cobbett's return to England in 1800, when Pitt and
Canning were also present. Hammond later transmitted
to Cobbett the Government's offer to set him up as editor
and proprietor of a Government subscribed newspaper.
See *Political Register* 4/4/1817, and my *Life of Cobbett*, p. 70. Hammond was then Under-Secretary for
Foreign Affairs in Pitt's Government. He was one of the
group, headed by Canning and Frere, which was responsible for the *Anti-Jacobin.*

    Mr. Claypoole. The Claypooles were pioneers under
Penn and leading men in Pennsylvania. This Claypoole
was a newspaper-proprietor with whom Cobbett had
several passages. See *Porcupine's Works*, vol. vii. p. 18 and
vol. xii. p. 105.

P. 58. *Mr. Swanwick.* See Note to p. 34.

P. 60. *Citizen Hint.* The signature attached to the letter
printed on page 71.

NOTES TO "THE SCARE-CROW"

P. 65. This piece was first published by Cobbett at Philadelphia in 1796, and re-issued in England. It is reprinted in *Porcupine's Works*, vol. iv.

P. 69. *M'Kean.* Thomas McKean (1734-1817) signed the
American Declaration of Independence, and was a leading Democratic member of Congress. In 1772 he was
Speaker of the House of Representatives, and from 1774
to 1783 a member of the Continental Congress. In 1777
he became Chief Justice of Pennsylvania and in 1799
Governor of the State. In 1797 Cobbett was tried before

him for libels on the King of Spain and the Spanish
Minister, who was McKean's father-in-law. Despite a
violent charge by McKean, the grand jury threw out the
bill by a majority of one. Cobbett then attacked McKean
savagely in a pamphlet, *The Democratic Judge* (re-published in England as *The Republican Judge*). McKean's
election as State Governor was one of the chief reasons
for Cobbett's leaving Philadelphia in 1799, when he was
engaged in his libel action with Dr. Benjamin Rush. See
my *Life of Cobbett*, p. 62. *The Democratic Judge* is reprinted in vol. vii. of *Porcupine's Works*, and there are
attacks on him throughout the later volumes.

    Ankerstrom. J. J. Anckerstroem—the Swedish noble
conspirator who assassinated Gustavus III. in 1792, and
was executed.

P. 71. *Mr. Vicesimus Knox.* Vicesimus Knox (1752-1821),
editor of *Elegant Extracts* and *Elegant Epistles* and head-
master of Tonbridge Grammar School, also wrote and
published anonymously in 1794, *The Spirit of Despotism*, a
Radical tract, which was re-issued later by William Hone
with the author's name.

P. 74. *Citizen Joseph Fauchet.* Baron Antoine Joseph Fauchet
was a leading Girondin. He was French Minister to
the United States from 1794 to 1796. Cobbett made
many attacks upon him. See *Porcupine's Works*, vol. i. p.
279, vol. ii. p. 370, and 396, etc.

P. 81. *Lepelletier.* Louis-Michel Lepelletier de Saint Fargeau
(1760-1793) was one of the noble representatives of Paris
in the National Assembly, and at first sided against the
people. Suddenly changing sides in 1789, he became a
strong revolutionary, and was one of the foremost in
urging the King's execution. On the eve of this event he
was assassinated in a restaurant by a former soldier of the
Royal Guard.

P. 82. *Mr. Carey.* See Note to page 43.
    Mr. Franklin Bache. See Note to page 12.
    Peter Pindar. i.e. John Wolcot (1738-1819), the satirist,
whose works include *Odes to Mr. Paine*, and other satires
on Radical leaders.

P. 87. *The Aurora.* The Baches' newspaper. See Note to
    p. 12.

NOTES TO "REMARKS OF THE PAMPHLETS LATELY PUBLISHED AGAINST PETER PORCUPINE"

P. 91. This piece was first published, following Cobbett's scurrilous *Life of Thomas Paine*, in Number v. of *The Political Censor* (September, 1796). It is reprinted in *Porcupine's Works*, vol. iv.

P. 96. *Randolph's Defence.* Edmund Jennings Randolph (1753-1813) was successively Governor of Virginia, Attorney-General of the United States, and Secretary of State, in which office he succeeded Jefferson in 1794. Fauchet, the French Ambassador (see Note to page 74), mentioned him in a dispatch sent home to France as having suggested that a discreet expenditure of money among American politicians would be likely to advance the French cause. This dispatch was captured and published, and Randolph had to resign. He published a defence of his conduct under the title of *Randolph's Vindication*, and to this Cobbett wrote a reply entitled *An Analysis of Randolph's Vindication* (1795). This will be found in *Porcupine's Works*, vol. ii. It should be noted that Fauchet disclaimed the meaning which had been put on his words, and corrected his view of Randolph in a later dispatch. Randolph was, in fact, vindicated, despite Cobbett's partisan eloquence.

Maddison. i.e. James Madison, the Democratic leader and later President of the United States.

Gallatin. Albert Gallatin (1761-1849) was born in Geneva. He became in youth an ardent republican, and emigrated to the United States in 1780. After some adventures, he settled in Philadelphia, profited by land speculation, and became a leading Democratic politician. He took an active part in settling the Whiskey Insurrection (see Note to page 45). In Congress, he was a follower of Madison, and became Secretary to the Treasury in 1801.

Swanwick. See Note to page 34.

P. 98. *Moreau.* This is presumably the same Moreau de Saint Mery whose book on Santo Domingo Cobbett had translated. See Note to page 50.

P. 100. *Hamilton.* Presumably Alexander Hamilton.

Belknap. Presumably Jeremy Belknap (1744-1798), a leading Congregational Minister of Boston. He wrote a

History of New Hampshire, and was a leading opponent of the slave trade.

Morse. Either Jedidiah Morse (1761-1826), a leading Congregationalist and father of the inventor, or Ebenezer Morse (? -1802) another minister of the same denomiination, who was noted for his pro-English views.

P. 101. *Samuel F. Bradford.* See Note to page 14.

P. 102. *Dr. Green.* This is probably Dr. Ashbel Green (1762-1848), pastor of the Presbyterian Church in Philadelphia and Professor of Mathematics and Natural Philosophy at Princeton.

The late Attorney-General, i.e. William Bradford. See Note to page 14.

P. 103. *Mr. Wolcot.* Oliver Wolcott (1760-1833) succeeded Hamilton as Secretary of the Treasury in 1795. He was later a leading banker.

P. 104. *Mr. Thornton.* Sir Edward Thornton (1766-1852) went to America as Secretary to George Hammond. In 1796 he became Secretary to the Legation at Washington, and he was Chargé d'Affaires from 1800 to 1804.

" *The language-maker.*" This Thornton was an early advocate of simplified spelling. He proposed to add a number of new letters to the alphabet, chiefly by printing the old ones upside down. His object was to cleanse the American language of European impurities as the Revolution had cleansed the American Constitution. Cobbett attacked him in *Porcupine's Gazette.* See *Porcupine's Works*, vol. ii. p. 53 and vol. vii. p. 209.

Dr. Andrews. John Andrews (1746-1813), who was head of the Episcopal Academy in Philadelphia, and Professor of Moral Philosophy in the University of Pennsylvania.

Mr. Bisset, Mr. Lewis. There are too many possible Bissets and Lewises for identification to be attempted.

Mr. Sedgewick. Probably Theodore Sedgwick (1747-1813), Judge of the Supreme Court of Massachusetts, and a leading Federalist.

Dr. Smith. William Smith, D.D. (1727-1803), first Provost of the College of Philadelphia. John Adams described him as " soft, polite, adulating, sensible, learned, industrious and indefatigable," and wrote of him, " This is one of the many irregular and extravagant characters of the age. I never heard one single person speak well of anything about him but his abilities, which are generally allowed to be good." Smith was pro-English during the

Revolution, but subsequently did his best to ingratiate himself with the victors.

P. 114. *Mr. Dallas.* Alexander James Dallas (1759-1817), a leading Philadelphia lawyer. He became Secretary of the State of Pennsylvania in 1791, and was later Secretary to the Treasury under Madison in 1814. Cobbett had many passages with him. See *Porcupine's Works*, vol. iv. p. 281, *et passim.*

P. 115. *Marten's Law of Nations.* Cobbett's translation of this work, first issued by Bradford in Philadelphia, was often reprinted in England.

P. 116. *New Year's Gift.* See Note to page 49.

Randall. Robert Randall was a land speculator, who was arrested for attempting to bribe members of Congress in order to secure concessions of land in the area of the Great Lakes. For his case, see *Porcupine's Works*, vol. iii. pp. 45 and 54.

NOTES TO "TALLEYRAND A SPY"

P. 120. This piece first appeared as an article in *Porcupine's Gazette,* the newspaper with which Cobbett followed up *The Political Censor,* in May, 1797. It is reprinted in vol. v. of *Porcupine's Works,* page 360.

Talleyrand. Charles Maurice de Talleyrand-Périgord (1754-1838), after supporting the Revolution in its earlier stages, and spending some time in England as a sort of unofficial ambassador, fled from France after the overthrow of the monarchy and the September massacres. He came to England, but was expelled, and went to the United States towards the end of 1793. He was then proscribed as an émigré ; but after the fall of the Jacobins the situation changed, and he was able to return to France at the end of 1795. In 1797 he became Foreign Minister. He was made Bishop of Autun in 1789, and was one of the few bishops who accepted the Civil Constitution of the Clergy. But in 1791 he resigned his bishopric, and devoted himself wholly to secular affairs.

P. 121. *New Year's Gift.* See Note to page 49.

P. 122. *Webster. i.e.* Noah Webster (1758-1843), who had published his *Grammatical Institute of the English Language* in 1783-5.

Thornton. The "language-maker." See Note to page 104.

Adet. Pierre Auguste Adet (1763-1832) was French

Minister to the United States after Fauchet. It fell to him to deliver the celebrated note of the Directory, accusing the United States Government of breach of neutrality and violation of the treaty of 1778. The issue of *The Political Censor* for November, 1796, is largely devoted to abuse of Adet and his work in America. After the note mentioned above, Adet suspended his functions as Minister, and returned to France, where he occupied administrative posts under Napoleon. He was also a chemist of some note.

P. 123. *Precious confessions.* The phrase is quoted from Fauchet's intercepted dispatch. (See Note to page 96.) Fauchet there wrote, " Besides, the precious confessions of Mr. Randolph alone throw a satisfactory light on every thing that came to pass." The question arose whether this meant that Randolph had been giving away State secrets to the French Minister. Randolph denied this, and Fauchet explained that " as to the communications which Mr. Randolph has made to me at different times, they were only of *opinions*, the greater part, if not the whole, of which I have heard *circulated as opinions*." Cobbett, in his reply, made great play with the original phrase. " What idea do the words *precious confessions* carry to our minds ? What is a confession? An *acknowledgement* which some one is *prevailed on* to make. And in what sense do we ever apply the epithet *precious*, but in that of *valuable, rare, costly*, or *dear*? Would any man that knows the meaning of those words, apply them to designate the common chat of a town, mere news-paper topics? We say, for instance, *precious stones*; but do we mean by these the rocks that we see cover the lands, or the flints and pebbles that we kick along the road? If some impudent quack were to tell us, that the pavement of Philadelphia is composed of *precious stones*, should we not hurl them at his head; should we not lapidate him? " (*A New Year's Gift to the Democrats* (1796), republished in *Porcupine's Works*, vol. ii. p. 422.)

NOTES TO "FAREWELL TO AMERICA"

P. 124. This piece is reprinted from *Porcupine's Works*, vol. xii. p. 108.

The Porcupine. On his return to England, after refusing the offer of the Government to set him up as editor of a subsidised newspaper (see page 143 and note thereto), Cobbett attempted to publish a daily paper of his own, under the name of *The Porcupine*. The first number appeared on October 30, 1800; but his resources soon proved unequal to the strain, and in November he sold the paper through John Gifford to Redhead Yorke, and it was incorporated in *The True Briton*. *The Porcupine* continued the policy which Cobbett had followed in America. It was violently hostile to France, and pronouncedly Jingo. It was after this failure that Cobbett, with the aid of William Windham, established *The Political Register*, which he continued to edit for the rest of his life.

P. 126. *Democracy and Federalism. i.e.* the two great American parties. Cobbett had by this time quarrelled almost as thoroughly with the Federalists as with the Democrats.

Five thousand dollars at a time. This is a reference to the great Rush libel action, which was the real cause of Cobbett's leaving the United States. Dr. Benjamin Rush (1745-1813) was a leading Philadelphia doctor and a Democratic member of Congress. He introduced a special treatment by " purging and bleeding " for the yellow fever. Cobbett, moved perhaps more by political than by medical animus, denounced him as a " poisonous trans-atlantic quack," and in his periodical writings assailed him with a spate of scurrilous abuse. Rush thereupon brought a libel action in the Supreme Court of Pennsylvania, and Cobbett, fearing the hostility of the State Governor, McKean, and his successor as Chief Justice, Shippen, tried to get the case removed to the Federal Courts. On one pretext after another, the hearing was delayed, Cobbett alleging that the motive was to embarrass him and to procure a packed jury. At length, in December 1799 judgment was given against him for five thousand dollars, and his effects in Philadelphia were seized in payment. On the day on which judgment was given, George Washington, who had been under Rush's treatment, died. Cobbett, who had by this time removed to New York, accused Rush of being responsible for his murder, and began, in 1800, a new paper, *The Rush-light*, in which he renewed his onslaughts on Dr. Rush. America soon became too hot to hold him, and he sailed for England, with this parting shot.

NOTES TO "THE COURT-MARTIAL"

P. 127. This piece originally appeared in *Cobbett's Weekly Political Register* of June 17, 1809. It there formed part of an open letter *To the Independent People of Hampshire,* on the subject of *The Court-Martial.* At that time Cobbett was already in violent opposition to the Government, and an attempt was made to discredit him by issuing in pamphlet form a garbled and selected account of the abortive court-martial proceedings here described. The full title of this pamphlet is as follows :—*Proceedings of a General Court Martial held at the Horse-Guards, on the 24th and 27th of March,* 1792, *for the trial of Capt. Richard Powell, Lieut. Christopher Seton, and Lieut. John Hall, of the 54th Regiment of Foot ; On several Charges preferred against them respectively by William Cobbett, Late Serjeant-Major of the said Regiment.* London. J. Gold. 1809. I have omitted from this reprint the controversial parts of the letter, in which Cobbett answered the specific charges made in the pamphlet, and have given only his connected account of what occurred. The piece as here printed is, however, continuous, and has not been altered or abridged in any way, save by the omission of a connecting particle in the opening sentence. In the original this reads, " The object of my *thus* quitting the army." It is immediately preceded by the letter from Lord Edward Fitzgerald and the Army Order already quoted in *The Life and Adventures of Peter Porcupine* (see page 36).

P. 128. *Dundas's system.* Sir David Dundas, Commander in Chief of the British Army from 1809, when he succeeded the Duke of York, to 1811. The General Regulations of 1792 were founded on his book, *Principles of Military Movements* (1788), in which he largely followed the methods of Frederick the Great.

P. 131. *Sir George Yonge.* Yonge (1731-1812) was Secretary for War from 1782 to 1783 and from 1783 to 1794. He was later Master of the Mint and Governor of Cape Colony, a post in which he was superseded for misgovernment in 1801.

P. 132. 200 *guineas.* A hundred and fifty guineas of this are connected with Cobbett's love affairs. See page 149.

The Judge-Advocate. Sir Charles Gould (1726-1806), Judge-Advocate General. Some of Cobbett's correspondence with him over this affair is printed in Lewis

Melville's *Life and Letters of William Cobbett*, vol. i. pp. 61 ff.

P. 133. *Letter to Pitt.* See Lewis Melville, *op. cit.*, vol. i. p. 62.

P. 137. *Suspension of Habeas Corpus.* The Habeas Corpus Act was suspended in 1794, as part of Pitt's campaign of repression against the Corresponding Societies and other working-class and reform organisations. It was also suspended in 1796, and again in 1798, in connection with the disturbances in Ireland and the Nore Mutiny.

NOTES TO "A RETROSPECT"

P. 139. This piece was originally published in *Cobbett's Weekly Political Register* of February 19, 1820, where it forms part of an open letter *To the Reformers, on the subject of raising a sum of money for the purpose of defraying the expences attending the securing of a seat in Parliament at the next Election.* I have extracted the entire section describing Cobbett's career up to his return to England in 1800.

Tale of a Tub. Cobbett was throughout his life fond of quoting Swift, who had more influence on his style than any other writer.

P. 140. *The present king. i.e.* George IV.

P. 142. *General Carleton.* Sir Guy Carleton, afterwards Lord Dorchester (1724-1808), served under Amherst at Quebec, and was made Governor of Quebec in 1772. His defence of Quebec in the American War was largely responsible for preserving the British dominion in Canada. In 1781 Carleton became commander in America, and in 1786 he was created Governor of Quebec, Nova Scotia, and New Brunswick, and raised to the peerage.

P. 143. *A Court-Martial.* See page 137 and Note.

The king's minister. i.e. George Hammond. See Note to page 53.

Reward was offered me. See Note to page 124.